SKIP COLLEGE,
START PROGRAMMING

SKIP COLLEGE, START PROGRAMMING

The Complete How-To Guide to Teaching Yourself
Software Development

ISBN   978-1-61961-689-9   Paperback

        978-1-61961-690-5   Ebook

SKIP COLLEGE, START PROGRAMMING

The Complete How-To Guide to
Teaching Yourself Software Development

SAM HINTON

CONTENTS

Dedication

This book is dedicated to my eager engineers and MBA buddies who are interested in learning the fundamentals of software development and asked me to write this instructional book. The book is also dedicated to my wife, Nola, who encouraged and supported me during the entire process.

ACKNOWLEDGMENTS

Thanks to the entire *Book In A Box* crew, especially Zach Obront (who was my first contact at Book In A Box), Brad Kauffman and Doug Watson, who advised me to start with this book, among others that I intend to write. My special thanks to Holly Maria Hudson, who guided and assisted me in creating a professional outline and table of contents for this book. I also thank the publishing manager, Julie Stubblefield, who coordinated between me and Holly Maria Hudson while we prepared the outline. My special thanks to Alex Hughes, who acted as editor and made sure that the audience of this book understands my intended message. How can I forget Dan Bernitt, the publisher who coordinated between Alex Hughes and I, who guided and assisted me in staying on the right track and getting my book published and available to the whole world. Dan, thank you very much for your time and concern.

Finally, thanks to my wife, Nola, who mentioned and introduced me to the BIAB group website (her inquisitive nature always keeps her aware of what's available to me). My special thanks also go to my college mates and friends (engineering and MBA buddies), who gave me the idea to teach the Software Development process through classes, which eventually led to writing this book. I hope this book will be of use to you all.

INTRODUCTION

I wrote this book because I've met many professionals outside the IT (information technology) field who are eager to learn and understand the concepts behind software development. Over several consulting assignments with companies that train IT and non-IT professionals with IBM, Oracle and Microsoft products, I realized that many trainees who don't have a programming background, find it extremely difficult to understand the content of the training materials because they lack a basic knowledge of computer programming. In some cases, I organize Saturday classes to teach the fundamental concepts and basic elements of computer programming to assist trainees. I also have lots of non-IT professional college mates and friends who ask me to teach them software development by organizing classes. This made me realize that there may be many people out there with a similar thirst for acquiring basic, fundamental knowledge for software development processes. So, instead of organizing classes for teaching and training, I chose to write this book so that anyone with a similar desire can access this valuable information.

Under normal circumstances, to become a computer programmer (software developer), you need a two-year associate's degree in Computer Programming or a four-year bachelor's degree in Computer Science or Software Engineering. But, there are other non-IT professionals with different academic disciplines who are knowledgeable enough to understand the basics of software development without going back to college, if they have access to the right learning materials. This book can help you understand what a programming language is, and how to use a programming language to create a software product (i.e. application system), because every application system is written by a programming language. The book includes many practical examples to teach you computer programming, and can serve as a comprehensive guide for teaching yourself software development without following a formal course of study or pursuing a college degree.

I am very glad that you have selected this book to start understanding the basics of a programming language and how to write a computer program (i.e. software). If you have any feedback, concerns, or questions after reading this material, feel free to contact me at *support@asiotech.net* or visit *http://www.asiotech.net/subscribe* to register and view frequently asked questions and their answers, and to post your questions as well.

BOOK AUDIENCE

This book is primarily intended for any non-IT professional (e.g., engineers, MBAs) who wants to switch careers and become a computer programmer/software developer, to work in the information technology field without going back to college. The book can also be useful to anyone else who wants to do the same, but doesn't want to go to college. Reading this book will enable them to begin coding or building software on their own.

IT professionals with obsolete software development methodologies working with programming languages like COBOL, Fortran, C, Pascal, etc., who now want to learn object-oriented programming to update their software development methodologies to enable them to develop modern Windows, Internet and mobile applications will also benefit by reading this book. Microsoft C#.NET programming language is used in this book to teach the reader how to write a computer program. The usage of C#.NET thoroughly explains the concepts and practices of object-oriented programming that allows for the creation of modern Windows, Internet and mobile applications.

BOOK ORGANIZATION STRUCTURE

This book is organized into four parts. Each part covers different, unique topics. The parts are arranged as follows:

PART ONE

This part introduces computer programming and explains what makes the computer work. Here you will learn the meaning and functionality of most common software, such as the operating system, compilers, etc., that collaborates with a computer program to make an application system function. Different types of programming paradigms (i.e. procedural or functional, and object-oriented programming) are thoroughly described. This part provides the characteristics of almost all programming languages, and uses Microsoft C#.NET programming language as a case study to teach you how to write a computer program. The Microsoft Visual Studio Software Development Environment tools and the .NET Framework Class Library functionalities to support object-oriented programming are also thoroughly explained.

PART TWO

This part introduces the application system development process. It explains the various parts that should be available before a software product can be developed. It explains all the necessary processes needed before an application system can be functional. It describes systems analysis and design, hardware platforms, operating systems, programming languages, coding (i.e., program writing), testing, implementation/deployment, software development environment tools etc., that support the overall goal of application system development.

PART THREE

This part introduces computer program and data access. Every application system uses some type of data. How data is accessed and saved by a program is thoroughly explained. Two of the most common data access methods (the File System and the Relational Database Management System) are explained with extensive practical examples.

PART FOUR

This part explains different types of most common programming. Console programming which replaced the first key-punch/paper programming method is explained with practical examples. Windows programming, which is the most common programming style in most organizations today, is explained with practical examples. Internet programming, which allows us to surf the web, is explained with a basic and practical example.

This part concludes the book with a summary of the knowledge the reader has acquired after reading the book and the potential benefits available to the reader.

PROGRAM EXAMPLES SOURCE CODE

To become a computer programmer (i.e., a software developer), you should be ready to code. Coding is extremely time consuming, but coding is where the programmer uses logic to instruct and control the computer machine. So if you want to know and understand how the examples in this book work, then I suggest you code everything exactly in your Visual Studio Development Environment.

On the other hand, if you don't have time to code, then you can visit the following website *http://www.asiotech.net/subscribe* to register for a free download of the source codes for the example program files. You can then copy and paste the codes into your Visual Studio Development Environment.

SYSTEM REQUIREMENTS

Before you can use the examples in this book, and also continue to write your own sample programs, you will need the following application system development environment:

- Hardware: Personal Computer (PC) – Desktop or Laptop

- Operating System: Microsoft Windows 7 and up

- Development Environment: Microsoft Visual Studio Express 2010 and up

- Programming Language: Microsoft C#.NET Express 2010 and up

- Relational Database Management System (RDBMS): Microsoft SQL Server 2008 Express and up

To download Microsoft Visual Studio Express 2010 and up, and C#.NET Express 2010 and up, for Console and Windows programming examples, follow these guidelines:

1. Search/Google for **"free visual studio 2010 express download"**

2. Select/Click on **"Download Visual Studio 2010 express and .NET Framework…"** and follow the download instruction. Make sure the link/URL for this download starts as *www.microsoft.com/en-us/…*

3. When asked "**Do you want to run or save ...**" at the bottom of the screen, select/click on "**run**" to download and install the software product.

To download Microsoft Visual Web Developer Express 2010 and up, for internet programming example in this book, follow these guidelines:

1. Search/Google for "**free visual web developer 2010 express download**"

2. Select/Click on any of the "**Download Visual Web Developer 2010 express ... free**" links/URL and follow the download instruction.

3. When asked "**Do you want to run or save ...**" at the bottom of the screen, select/click on "**run**" to download and install the software product.

To download Microsoft SQL Server 2008 Express and up, follow these guidelines:

1. Search/Google for "**sql server 2008 express free download**"

2. Select/Click on "**Download Microsoft SQL Server 2008 Express from official...**" and follow the download instruction.

3. When asked "**Do you want to run or save ...**" at the bottom of the screen, select/click on "**run**" to download and install the software product.

Note that Microsoft Windows 7, Microsoft Visual Studio, Microsoft C#, Microsoft Visual Web Developer and Microsoft SQL Server are all trademarks of the Microsoft Corporation.

PART I

INTRODUCING COMPUTER PROGRAMMING

This part introduces computer programming and explains what makes the computer work. Here you will learn the meaning and functionality of most common software, such as the operating system, compilers, etc., that collaborates with a computer program to make an application system function. Different types of programming paradigms (i.e. procedural or functional, and object-oriented programming) are thoroughly described. This part provides the characteristics of almost all programming languages, and uses Microsoft C#.NET programming language as a case study to teach you how to write a computer program. The Microsoft Visual Studio Software Development Environment tools and the .NET Framework Class Library functionalities to support object-oriented programming are also thoroughly explained.

CHAPTER 1

HOW DO COMPUTERS WORK?

Like any other machine, computers are designed for a purpose. Airplanes are machines just like computers, and they were designed to allow pilots and passengers to get from point "a" to point "b" more quickly. Similarly, computers were designed to save time and make people's lives easier. They achieve this by accepting and manipulating data to help the user reach a goal. This data is made up of strings of characters and numbers that can be processed according to a sequence of instructions (known as a computer program). This allows computers to work with many data formats, including: text, images, audio, and video.

To achieve all of this, a computer uses a sophisticated system of software applications that work together to perform operations and execute commands. It includes the operating system, compiler, interpreter, application programs, programming languages, and more. Of course, you also need a computer programmer to make all of this happen.

THE SOFTWARE THAT MAKES COMPUTERS WORK

Since this book was written to teach you how to use a programming language to write your own software, it's important that you understand how the computer's native software collaborates with the software you'll write (i.e., your program). So, let's see how the computer's major software systems work alongside you, the programmer, to make programs work.

PROGRAMMING LANGUAGE

Just like the English language allows a supervisor to give instructions to his employees, a programming language lets the programmer give instructions to the computer. This creates a means of communicating with the computer that can be used to control its behavior. But, before any of that can happen, you must first learn to speak its language.

Unlike human languages, programming languages are designed and implemented by computer scientists at colleges, universities, or software manufacturing labs. For example, FORTRAN was originally developed/invented by the Department of Computer Science at University of Waterloo (Ontario in Canada). Java was invented by a computer scientist named James Arthur Gosling, C++ was created by a computer science research professor named Bjarne Stroustrup, and Microsoft's C# programming language was designed and created at a Microsoft laboratory by a group of computer scientists and software engineers from the .NET research group.

OPERATING SYSTEM

An operating system, or OS, is a computer program. It's the most important piece of software on a computer because it never sleeps, even when the computer is off; that's why some call it the "resident software manager." The operating system places applications on a device and prepares the environment with which the user will interact when the computer is turned on. It manages both the hardware and software resources and provides common services for computer programs.

A computer is useless without an operating system, because programs can't run and provide results without the assistance and guidelines of the operating system. Usually, many different types of programs will run simultaneously on a computer, even if you can't see them all. For instance, you can edit a document in a word processor while listening to music. All of these programs need access to the computer's CPU (central processing unit), memory, storage, and at times, peripherals like printers, scanners, or cameras. The operating system coordinates all of this to make sure that each program gets what it needs.

It's also worth mentioning that operating systems are always written for a specific hardware system. For instance, IBM's OS/400 is written for the AS/400 mini-computer series, while Windows and Mac OS X are written for personal computers, and Android and iOS are written for mobile devices. Linux (which is a descendant of UNIX) is currently the only exception to this rule. UNIX was originally developed at AT&T Bell Laboratories Research Center in New Jersey for the DEC VAX PDP mini-computer systems series. Since Linux is a collaborative effort by programmers from several companies, no one company owns it and it can be used on nearly any device, from a watch, to a microwave, to a super computer.

The hardware you buy, whether it's a smartphone or a desktop computer, will come with a preloaded operating system. But, at times you can replace the OS with a different one.

COMPILER

Humans use letters, numbers, and symbols to communicate with each other. Programming languages use these same characters to communicate instructions to computers. But unlike humans, computers don't speak our language and can't even read our characters (e.g., a – z, A – Z, $, #, & etc., and 0 – 9). So, programming language designers, create something called a compiler. The compiler's duty is to make sure that the program obeys all the syntax laws of the programming language and also convert program instructions into a language that the computer understands. This language is known as machine language, which uses a binary arithmetic, or "base two", approach.

Just like a human couldn't read a coded message without first decoding it, a computer can't read a programming language without a compiler. Because of this, every programming language comes with its own unique compiler that understands the programming language and can convert it to binary. For instance, Java has its own unique compiler while C# has another unique compiler.

The first thing that a compiler does is check that the program has obeyed all the laws of the language it was written in. If the program passes the test, then the compiler will transform the characters into their binary form (i.e., zeros and ones) to create an executable program. Some compilers, such as the C# compiler, will convert C# code into an intermediary language, usually an assembly language so that another compiler will convert it to a machine language. This allows one programming language to run on many different hardware systems.

INTERPRETER

The interpreter is another unique program that converts a programming language into intermediary code. But, unlike the compiler, which goes through the entire program before reporting syntax errors, the interpreter checks for errors line by line and stops when it finds one. The error must then be fixed for the interpreter to continue converting the code.

Because of the unique way an interpreter works, it's slower than a compiler and exposes software to viruses and other attacks. One programming language that commonly uses an interpreter is JavaScript, which is used with HTML in web browsers.

TRANSLATOR

A translator is a program that takes an application program written in one language and converts it into another language without changing the functional or logical structures of the original code. The translator can take machine language code and turn it into a programming language, and vice versa.

Compilers and interpreters are both types of translators. For instance, if the translator converts a program written in a high-level programming language into another high-level programming language (i.e., C# to Java) this is called a source-to-source translator. If it translates a high-level programming language into a lower-level machine language code that's meant to be executed, it's called a compiler. If it translates a high-level programming language into an intermediary code, such as an assembly language, to be immediately executed, it's called an interpreter.

MACHINE LANGUAGE

Machine languages are the only languages that computers can understand. They're the lowest- level programming languages that computers can use to execute programs. Machine languages use a binary format that communicates through zeros and ones. Therefore, it's very difficult for humans to write or even understand machine language. That's why compilers, interpreters, and translators are used, because they can generate the machine code during the translation process.

Programmers will either use a high-level programming language or an assembly language when providing the computer with instructions. Assembly languages contain the same instructions as a machine language, but the instructions and variables have names instead of just binary numbers. This allows us to write machine instructions in the same way you would if you were using a high-level programming language (but, more efficiently by using less code).

Machine language code is made up of instructions that are directly executed by the CPU (central processing unit). Each instruction performs a very specific task, such as looping, jumping, or arithmetic logical operation on a unit of data in a CPU registry or memory. Every CPU has a unique machine language; therefore, programs must be rewritten or recompiled to run on different types of computers.

DEVICE DRIVERS

Device drivers are special programs that allow your computer to interact with peripheral devices, such as a printer, screen, or camera. This driver provides a software interface for the device, allowing the operating system and other programs to access hardware functions without needing to know the precise details of the hardware being used.

Device drivers are hardware dependent and operating system specific. This means that a driver's computer programs are written for a specific piece of hardware and a specific operating system. For instance, a device driver written for Windows wouldn't work on a device using a Linux OS, and vice versa.

APPLICATION PROGRAM

An application program is software written to instruct the computer to solve a real-world problem on behalf of the user. Without application programs, the computer would be a useless invention. Some application programs include ones designed to control the departure and arrival of flight, robot systems, nuclear bomb control systems, etc.

DIFFERENT KINDS OF COMPUTER PROGRAMMERS

After you finish reading this book, you'll be able to write your own computer program. So, it's important to introduce you, the aspiring computer programmer, to the types of programs you may end up developing.

Software systems, or computer programs, are generally grouped into two main categories: systems programs and application programs. Systems programs focus on maximizing the computer's internal capabilities, while application programs focus on how the computer can solve real-world problems. These two areas are handled by system programmers and application programmers, respectively. Let's take a look at each one's responsibilities.

SYSTEM PROGRAMMER

System programmers are responsible for developing computer systems software, such as the operating system, device drivers, firmware, network support software products, etc. These programmers write software that prepares the environment for developing and running applications. For instance, they may write software development kits (SDK), tools for fine-tuning your computer's performance, programs for handling network issues and supporting remote program development, database management systems, intranet/Internet server performance issues, and more.

These programmers develop the software that the computer needs to perform its tasks in the most efficient and reliable way possible, with minimal technical issues. They'll usually be found working in the lab of a software manufacturer like IBM or Microsoft. Some companies may also use system programmers to manage their local area network and provide overall computer system administration. In these cases, they'll usually be identified as systems engineers, network engineers, or systems administrators.

APPLICATION PROGRAMMER

Application programmers, develop real-life applications like banking, insurance, or airline reservation systems. Their work will involve any type of real-world application where a user will ask the computer to complete a task on their behalf.

The focus of their work is developing the software needed by users to perform their daily tasks in the most efficient and reliable way. These programmers can be found at any organization that uses computer systems as part of its day-to-day business, scientific, or engineering operations.

SOFTWARE DEVELOPER

A software developer is any computer programmer that writes computer programs. Therefore, both system and application programmers are software developers. This title has only come into use after colleges and universities introduced degree programs in software engineering. Usually, organizations will assign titles to programmers based on their years of experience or their specialty in the development process.

WHAT HAVE YOU LEARNED?

- A device's operating system allows it to run programs.

- Programs that are written in a programming language must be converted to machine language for the device to understand it.

- This conversion process is performed by one of three types of translators: a source-to-source translator, a compiler, or an interpreter.

- Device drivers allow your device to communicate with peripheral devices.

- Applications solve real-world problems and are the most frequently used software.

- There are two types of programmers. System programmers handle the systems that allow devices to function and run applications, and application programmers create software that can solve real-world problems.

CHAPTER 2

WHAT ARE PROGRAMMING LANGUAGES?

A programming language is just like any other language that humans use, it helps us to communicate. But, in this case you're communicating with a computer and not another person. Programming languages are also similar to human languages in many other ways. For example, English, French, and Chinese, all have syntax, semantics and grammar rules. In turn, this creates meaningful identifiers such as verbs, nouns, adjectives, and prepositions. Now with all of these components, the speaker can create meaningful phrases and sentences that communicate their message.

Programming languages are exactly the same. They have their own syntax, semantics, lexical structures, and data types. In order to communicate effectively, you must not only learn the programming language, but also abide by its rules. In this section, we'll explain what rules are commonly found across all programming languages.

SYNTAX

The first step in using a programming language is understanding its syntax. These are the rules that define how the program should be written in order to communicate with the machine. These define what sequences of characters can be used as an identifier to correctly structure a program. Each programming language has its own unique rules to adhere to. For instance, in C# an identifier can't start with a number (e.g., "myName" is legal, whereas "8myName" is illegal). But, remember that "8myName" could be acceptable in another programming language.

In a programming language, syntax generally describes how language variables and characters should be combined to create a legal computer program for that language. This is one of the reasons that each programming language is accompanied by its own unique compiler, to monitor syntax rules before conversion to machine language. Below, you can compare the basic syntax of a few programming languages:

C basic syntax	C# basic syntax
| ```c
#include <stdio.h>
#include <conio.h>
int main ()
{
    /* this line is for C comment */
    printf ("Hi, reader!");
    return 0;
}
``` | ```csharp
using System;
using System.Collections.Generic;
using System.Linq;
using System.Text;
namespace CommandLineApp
{
    class HelloReaderApp
    {
        static void Main(string[ ] args)
        {
            // this line is for one of C# comments
            Console.WriteLine ("Hi, reader!");
        }
    }
}
``` |
| Java basic syntax | VB.NET basic syntax |
| ```java
import java.io;
import java.util;
package CommandLineApp
{
    public class HelloReaderApp
    {
    public static void main(String[ ]  args) {
    /* this line is for java comment */
    System.out.println ("Hi, reader!");
      }
    }
}
``` | ```vbnet
Imports System
Module HelloReaderModule
    Sub Main()
        Console.WriteLine ("Hi, reader!")
    End Sub
End   Module
``` |

When compiling a written program (converting the source code into machine code), the compiler's first task, is to make sure that all of the languages syntax rules have been adhered to. The compiler then reports any syntax errors and won't continue with the conversion until all syntax errors have been corrected. So, the first thing you should look for in any programming language is what the syntax rules are. That way you can be sure that your program will be compiled into executable code that the computer can run.

SEMANTICS

In programming language theory, semantics refers to creating a statement or expression that follows the syntax of a programming language, just like a correct statement in a language like English must form a logical sentence. Unfortunately, the compiler can't detect semantic or logical errors, because there are no rules to govern semantics. But, if there's an incorrect statement or expression, it will create an illogical result. For instance, consider these C# program statements:

```
// I'm sample C# statement comments - I know the compiler will ignore me but that's ok
// because I already know the compiler won't process me
//                            - no comment -
Line-1:     int age, answer, result = 0;
Line-2:     string myTextMsg = "Hi, I want to be a Computer Programmer";
Line-3:     result = (age / myTextMsg);          // i.e. age divided by myTextMsg
//                           - end of sample C# statements -
```

These statements all use proper syntax since the identifiers (e.g., "age" and "answer") follow the syntax rules of C#. However, "Line-3" is semantically incorrect. In this case, the program will compile with warnings, such as "variable 'age' and 'answer' not initialized and variable 'answer' declared but not used." But when the program runs, the result value will be unknown since the "age" integer identifier is expecting another integer to perform the "divide" operation on; when it instead sees a "string" data type (i.e. "myTextMsg"). In these cases, the compiler will be confused. The following example shows code that uses correct syntax and semantics:

```
Line-1:     string myTextMsg = "Number of Students in each class ....";
Line-2:     int totalStudents = 250, numberOfClassrooms = 5, studentsPerClass = 0;
Line-3:     studentsPerClass = (totalStudents / numberOfClassrooms);
```

So, just like written and spoken communication must use different parts of speech to create a meaningful statement, programming must use correct syntax to create meaningful semantics. Because even though your program may still compile, you won't get the result you want unless it uses correct semantics.

In human language, semantics is the study of the meaning of phrases and sentence structures in a particular language. In programming language theory, semantics is the field of study focused on the meaning of programming languages. This requires evaluating the meaning of strings using correct syntax as defined by a specific programming language.

LEXICAL STRUCTURE

Lexical structure is what controls the correct usage of syntax, semantics, and data types in a programming language. It shows how the language represents data (e.g., strings or numbers) in machine code format. It's about the correct usage of data type values in the memory/storage, whether the programming language represents data using 16-bit, 32-bit or 64-bit code units for encoding. The lexical structure of the language is concerned with the maximum value that a data type can handle and the types of values that can be assigned to it. Usually, programming language designers will follow the standards set by ASCII, UTF encoding. For instance, Java represents text in sequences of 16-bit code units in UTF-16 encoding.

Lexical structure manages the usage of literal (the source code representation of a primitive data type value). For instance, in C# an integer literal may be expressed in decimal (base 10) or binary (base 2). The character literal is expressed as a character and must be enclosed in ASCII single quotes, while a string literal consisting of zero or more characters must be enclosed in ASCII double quotes. Here are a few examples of 'int', 'decimal', 'char' and 'string' data types literal declarations in C#:

```
// ----- the following are samples of C# literals statements
/* Line-1 is an integer whole number literal - Line-2 is an example of decimal number literal */
// Line-3 is an example of character literal and Line-4 is an example of string literal
//                          - no comment
Line-1: Integer literal:      int myWholeNumber = 2400;
Line-2: Decimal literal:      decimal myAccountBalance = 2400.80m;
Line-3: Character literal:    char alowercase = 'a', AupperCase = 'A';
Line-4: String literal:       string myTextMsg = "Hi, I want to be a Programmer";
//                      - no comment
//                      - end of literal/constant examples
```

The maximum values for a data type are provided by the programming language and the programmer must know the lexical structure of the language being used. Otherwise, you will lose data, especially in programs for financial, scientific, or engineering applications that use many mathematical formulas.

DATA TYPES

Data types are the different types of data that a programming language designer wants the language to be able to work with. Each programming language will have its own data types, even though most will also come with basic data types like "integer" and "character." A data type is a set of data values with predefined characteristics (e.g., their values, how they're stored, and what kinds of operations are performed on them). For example, an "integer" is a data type that can be used to store whole numbers and the basic operations for it are "addition," "subtraction," "multiplication," and "division."

At the time of writing this book, there are two basic data types that a programming language can work with, primitive and user-defined (based on computer science discipline). In the following sections we'll explain how these two data types are used and what their capabilities are.

PRIMITIVE DATA TYPES

Primitive data types are the most basic data types and are built into programming languages (e.g., Java, C++, C#). These basic data types are provided by the programming language as a building block for writing programs and are identified by a unique keyword that the compiler can read. These data types only have limited uses and the programmer has no control over what operations can or can't be performed on these primitive data types.

All primitive data types have a fixed size. For example, in Java the value of an integer data type is restricted to the numbers - 2,147,483,648 through + 2,147,483,647. In the same way, any primitive data type will have a limited range of values that applies across the programming language.

Primitive data types will also have a fixed list of operations. For example, the integer data type may only have basic mathematical operations, such as "addition," "subtraction," "multiplication," "division," and logical comparisons like "equal to." Textual primitive data types may have operations, such as "comparing two words," "joining characters to make words," "joining strings to make phrases or sentences," etc.

USER-DEFINED DATA TYPES

Because of limited functionalities of primitive data types, most modern programming languages offer a second data type, user-defined data types. These allow the programmer to create/define a data type and assign any number of operations to work on it. Allowing for more complicated composite data types to be created than would otherwise be possible with primitive data types.

User-defined data types usually model real-world object classifications, such as animals, trees, or vehicles, and they also allow for functions, such as interface, encapsulation, and inheritance. What does this all mean? For example, when you drive a car you don't have to understand how the engine's internal components make the car accelerate, you simply use the steering wheel and pedals. These are interfaces that allow you to more easily perform a complex task. In the same way, user-defined data types make performing complex tasks easier to perform by creating an interface.

Since the programmer can create their own data types, they can hide all of the operations that are done in the background from the user. Programs that make use of these data types can access functions through a special interface created by the programmer, without knowledge of how these functions work. This is the concept that makes it possible for applications to be digitized and used through networks from any part of the world. An example of this would be a web service, such as a banking interface. This service can be accessed by millions of users, and they are able to perform many complex functions through a simple interface.

VALUE TYPES

Since a computer program involves one or more functions exchanging data to accomplish a specific task, it's very important for the programmer to understand value types when passing parameters between functions. Most primitive data types are value types and the local variables in a function contain the actual value type and are allocated on a "stack" (i.e. stack of memory). For example, in C#, the integer "studentAge" and the floating number "studentGPA" are declared as follows:

```
int studentAge = 21;      // the value 21 is in the memory address identified as studentAge
float studentGPA = 3.5;   // the value 3.5 is in the memory location identified as studentGPA
```

A value type's lifetime is from the beginning of a function until the end when the "stack" is destroyed. If a value type is passed as a parameter to a function, whatever the function does to it won't change the original value type since it's a local copy. You can imagine this value type as a letter in the mailbox. It's the actual letter and not a note directing you to go find the letter at another place, such as the post office.

REFERENCE TYPES

All user-defined data types are reference types. At times, a primitive data type like a "string" in some languages may also be a reference type. Instances of reference types are also referred to as objects. Objects are allocated from the "heap" (available memory) and are accessed through reference variables.

Some compilers have a function known as the "garbage collector." This function goes through a heap of memory and deletes objects from the heap that have been inactive for a certain amount of time. Thus, leaving enough room for new objects to be created.

Since objects are passed as parameters to functions through reference variables, whatever modification does by the called function affects the original object value. You can think of a reference variable as a note in your mailbox that tells you where to go to find your mail.

PROCEDURAL-ORIENTED PROGRAMMING LANGUAGE

Procedural-oriented programming languages, or functional programming languages, are designed for data-driven (usually primitive data types) program execution. Program execution is based on sequential processing. This means that if the program needs to access a function or sub-routine to perform a task, execution will stop until the main program has control again and then it will continue to the next instruction. In most cases, program execution will only be interrupted due to a fatal error or at the end of the program.

These programming languages only come with built-in primitive data types and don't give the programmer the ability to create their own data types and operations. A few examples of this type of programming language are C, Pascal, FORTRAN, and COBOL. However, some of these are being updated to also include user-defined data types.

OBJECT-ORIENTED PROGRAMMING LANGUAGE

Object-oriented programming languages allow the programmer to create their own data types and operations. This includes languages like Smalltalk, C++, C#, and Java. This allows the programmer to model real-world objects (items), such as animals, rivers, vehicles, aircrafts, etc. Programs are created using instances of these objects, and program execution is based on their behavior (object-driven). In these languages, execution is non-sequential since objects can interrupt each other. An example of this type of program would be a Windows application that the user can control the behavior of the program through buttons and other user-control objects.

PROGRAMMING LANGUAGE CHARACTERISTICS

Programming language designers build their languages to use all or most of the following programming language characteristics. These language attributes are then combined to form a computer program. This means that aspiring computer programmers must understand how to use the programming language characteristics for the language they want to use. Now you'll go through a brief overview of the most common characteristics:

KEYWORDS

Keywords are predefined identifiers (names) that follow the syntax rules of a given programming language. Each language has its own unique keywords. These are identifiers that the compiler uses. The programmer shouldn't create identifiers with the same name as an existing keyword. Here are a few examples of C# programming language keywords:

```
int, decimal, float, double, char, string, struct, class, for, while, switch, if, property, return
```

ARITHMETICAL AND LOGICAL OPERATIONS IDENTIFIERS

Humans put their own logic into computers so that they can do things for them. Every programming language comes with arithmetical and logical operations identifiers (symbols) that the computer programmer can use to allow the computer to perform data processing. Below are a few examples of basic arithmetic and logical operators (symbols):

Operator identifier	Description
+	Addition operator (used by languages like C, C++, java, C# etc.)
==	Equal to operator (used by C#)
=	Equal to operator (used by C, C++, java, and many other languages)

VARIABLE DECLARATION

In computer science discipline, a variable has the same meaning and purpose as a variable in algebra (e.g., x, y, or z) in mathematics. Just like solving for x is important in algebra, variable declarations are extremely important in computer programming. When you declare a variable in a program, you're telling the compiler to request a memory location from the operating system for your program to use for processing. The value in a variable name isn't permanent because any value with the same data type can be placed in that variable by the programmer to instruct the computer. Some languages, such as C#, are case sensitive (e.g., the variable "studentFirstName" is different from "studentfirstName"). The following table shows a few examples of C# variable declarations:

Data Type	Purpose	Example with initial values
int	To store small integer whole numbers	int studentAge = 24, retirementAge = 65;
long	To store larger integer whole numbers	long totalMiles = (9000000 * 9000000)
decimal	To store money	decimal accountBalance = 248000.00;
float	To store short decimal point numbers	float mathOneFix = 1.1234567;
double	To store long decimal point numbers	double mathTwoFix = 1.123456789012345;
char	To store single characters	char dollarSign = '$', atSign = '@', charA = 'A';
string	To store strings/text messages	string employeeName = "Thomas Jamieson";
class	To create user-defined type	Students student = new Students ("Jim Doe");

It's good programming practice to always initialize variables so that the compiler doesn't have to provide default values for uninitialized declared variables. Also, omit any variables that you won't use for data processing since computer memory is very valuable in the current multitasking, multiprocessing and multithreading environment.

CONSTANT DECLARATION

A constant declaration is a declaration in a program that has an initial value that doesn't change during program execution. This type of declaration is extremely useful in scientific and engineering applications where fixed values are used to perform calculations based on formulas. Below you can see a few constant declarations in C#:

```
const int usEmployeeRetirementAge = 65;         // integer whole number constant declaration
const float studentGPA = 3.8;                   // short decimal number constant declaration
const double mathPie = 3.14159;                 // long decimal number constant  declaration
const char usCurrencySign = '$';                 // character constant declaration
const string companyName = "ASIO Technologies";  // string constant declaration
```

You'll notice that constant declarations always have initial values. Some languages, such as C#, will warn you if you declare a constant variable without initialization.

ASSIGNMENT STATEMENTS

Assignment statements are how values, expressions, or function call results are assigned to variables in a program. Different programming languages have different symbols or special characters to use for assignments. The C# programming language uses the "=" symbol to assign values to declared variables or constants. Below are a few examples:

Assignment statement declaration	Example of assignment statements

datatype variablename = value;
datatype constantname = fixed value;
variablename = expression;
variablename = function call return value;
	int total = 0, numOne = 7807, numTwo = 968;
	string firstName = "Joan", lastName = "Jamieson";
	double const mathPie = 3.1415924654;
	string fullName = (firstName + " " + lastName);
	total = addTwoNumbers (numOne, numTwo);

INPUT STATEMENTS

Input statements are used to gain access to data for processing. Below are a few examples of C# input statements:

```
System.Console.ReadLine ();        // a statement to receive input data from the command line
System.IO.File.ReadAllLines ();  // a statement to read records from the file system
SELECT                            // an SQL statement to retrieve a record from the database
```

OUTPUT STATEMENTS

Output statements are used to make information available to other programs, users, files, or databases. Below are a few examples of C# output statements:

```
System.Console.WriteLine ();        // a statement to display data on the command line
System.IO.File.WriteAllLines ();    // a statement to write records to a text file
INSERT                              // an SQL statement to add a record to the database
```

CONDITIONAL STATEMENTS

Conditional statements test for specific conditions and perform specific actions to see if the conditions are true or false. Below is a C# conditional statement format declaration:

'if' Conditional statement declaration	Example of the 'if' conditional statement

```if (condition is true)```
 ```{```
     ```perform this task```
 ```}```
 ```else```
     ```perform a different task```
	```if (studentGPA > 3.8)```
	 ```{```
	     ```MessageBox.Show ("You have a scholarship");```
	 ```}```
	 ```else```
	     ```MessageBox.Show ("Contact financial office");```

LOOPING STATEMENTS

Looping statements are used to create a loop that executes a statement for as long as a certain condition is true. Below is a C# looping statement format declaration:

'while' looping statement declaration format	Example of the 'while' looping statement

```while (condition is true)```
 ```{```
     ```continue to perform this task```
 ```}```
	```int totalRecords = 0;```
	 ```while (notEndofDatabaseRecords)```
	 ```{```
	     ```totalRecords = totalRecords + 1;```
	 ```}```

TRANSFER STATEMENTS

Transfer statements are used to transfer control from one instructional process execution to another location in the program based on logical evaluation conditions. The table below shows one of several C# transfer statement samples ("return" statement).

The "return" statement is used to return control back to a function call and/or to exit a loop based on specific testing conditions.

```
int addTwoNum ( int numOne, int numTwo)        int totalRecords = 0;
{                                              while   (notEndofDatabaseRecords)
    int total = (numOne +  numTwo);            {
    return total;                                  totalRecords = totalRecords +  1;
}                                                  if (fatalError)
                                                       return;  // go to where you came from
                                               }
```

COMMENT DECLARATION

Comment in a programming language is the identifier that the programmer uses to express the purpose of declarations for statements, expressions, functions, etc. Comment is very important in programming especially when writing large programs where several programmers are working on the same project. Comment syntax is a reserved word and is known and understood by the compiler only. Comments are not processed and executed by the compiler. The following example shows some deferent kinds of C# comments.

```
// I am a comment - so the compiler will not process me
/* I'm also a comment in C# too but C, C++ and java also use me */
/// I'm a comment in C#, you can use me to generate HTML pages
```

FUNCTIONS

A function is a very important concept in computer programming, just like f(x) in mathematics. A function performs a specific task. A computer program is nothing but one or more functions exchanging data and messages through parameters in order to complete a specific task (i.e., to create the programmer's desired result). In C#, functions are called "methods". Below are some of C# "method" declarations and examples:

```
return-datatype function-name (datatype1 variablename ...... datatypeN variablename)
{
    // place the operations to be performed by this function here
}
```

Function that doesn't return a value	Function that returns a value to the caller
```void addTwoNumbers (int nOne, int nTwo)\n{\n int total = 0;\n total = (nOne + nTwo);\n System.Console.WriteLine (total);\n}```	```int addTwoNumbers (int nOne, int nTwo)\n{\n int total = 0;\n total = (nOne + nTwo);\n return total;\n}```

The instructions that invoke the above functions will already have values in the "nOne" and "nTwo" integer variable parameters. The word "void" tells the C# compiler that this function does not return a value/result to the function caller.

DATA STRUCTURES/COLLECTIONS

Another important characteristic of programming languages that you should look for is how data structures (some languages, like Java and C# call these collections) are declared and used. In computer science, a data structure is a way of organizing data in the computer memory and storage devices, like a disc, so that it can be used efficiently. A data structure is a group of data elements grouped together under one identifier/name. These elements/items in the structure, usually known as members, can have the same data type with a fixed length or different data types with varying lengths.

Most common data structure types include: Structure/Record, Array, ArrayList, List, Linked List, File, Stack, Queue, and Tree. Usually a data structure is designed to organize data for a specific purpose so that it can be accessed and used correctly. Every programming language has functions to declare and use data structures. The following section provides some common data structures with sample declarations and uses.

STRUCTURE/RECORD

A structure or record is a data structure that consists of primitive data types grouped together under one identifier (name). As a matter of fact, structure was the beginning of the concept of user-defined data types even though most languages treat it as a primitive data type and let it live on the 'stack' memory allocation. Languages like C, C++, C# and Java call it structure; other languages like Pascal and obsolete languages like COBOL call it record. Modern languages like C# go to the extent of adding methods (functions) to enhance the capabilities and behavior of structure. Consider the following C# structure and and COBOL record declarations examples:

C# structure declaration format sample	COBOL record declaration format sample
```struct student{ int studentAge = 0; string studentName = " ";}```	```01 student-record. 05 studentAge 9 (2) VALUE 0. 05 studentName X (30) VALUE " ".```

To access the members of the "struct student" in C#, you have to declare a variable type of "student" (for instance "firstYearStudent"). This is how to access the 'studentAge' member of the C# student struct: *firstYearStudent.studentAge* and this is how to access the 'studentAge' member in the COBOL student record: *studentAge of student-record*.

ARRAY DECLARATION

An array is one of the most common and important data structures that you should look for in any programming language, because almost all programming languages come with the array data structure. You must therefore know how an array is declared and used in a programming language. In computer programming, an array is a data structure that groups same data types into several consecutive memory locations with one identifier (name). An array is a collection of variables belonging to the same data type with a fixed length (i.e., the number of memory location being requested by the programmer is fixed). Each item in the group is an element of the array and is accessed using an index. Different programming languages declare arrays differently. The following is how C# declares the array data type:

```
int [ ] studentsAges;                    // array declaration without initialization
int [ ] studentsAges = { 23, 22, 19, 20 }    // array declaration with four items
```

In C#, the items in the array are accessed through an index with 0 referring to the first item. That means you must use the following to access the first element in the array:

```
int firstStudentAgeInTheStudentsAgesArray = studentsAges [0];
```

The content of the integer variable *firstStudentAgeInTheStudentsAgesArray* will be 23.

ARRAYLIST DECLARATION

The 'ArrayList' data structure is an improvement on 'Array'. It allows different data types (objects) to be added to the list and doesn't have a fixed length. It also has certain basic functions that allow you to manage the list. Because the members are not guaranteed to be of the same data type, the programmer is responsible for type conversion. The following shows how to declare and use the 'ArrayList' data structure in C#:

```
ArrayList studentsNames = new ArrayList ();          // ArrayList declaration
studentsNames.Clear ();                       // initialize the students list to spaces
studentsName.Add ("James Corban");                     // add a student to the list
```

LIST DECLARATION

The 'List' is a type-safety data structure. That is, it forces all of the members in the list to have the same data type, to remove the burden of conversion. It has several functions to manage the list. Example 'Clear', 'Add', 'Remove', etc. The following shows how to declare 'List' data structure in C#:

```
List<T> sameDataTypeVariable = new List<T> ();            // where T stands for datatype
List<string> studentsNames = new List<string> ();   // list contains string values only
List<int> studentsAges = new List<int> ();          // list contains integer values only
List<employee> employees = new List<employee> ();    // list contains object values only
```

WHAT HAVE YOU LEARNED?

- Programming languages have the same characteristics as human languages.

- Syntax means that code must be written according to the rules, or grammar, of a programming language.

- Semantics means that the code can't just use correct syntax, it must also make sense and create a logical result.

- Lexical structure refers to the structure that a program's code must follow to be properly encoded.

- Data types refer to the information that the programming language is capable of recognizing and processing.

- Functions are the most important part of any program, because they produce the programmer's desired result.

CHAPTER 3

WHAT IS BASIC COMPUTER PROGRAMMING?

COMPUTER PROGRAMMING

Computer programming is the process of using a programming language to tell the computer to perform a specific task. For example, imagine that you want to write a program to monitor your spending habits. You'll need a programming language to write it with. Then, you'll need to understand and know how to use the syntax of the programming language that you want to use. You also need to know which software development environment you'll use to code, test, and deploy your application.

In this book, we'll use the Microsoft C# programming language to learn how to write programs and become a computer programmer. We'll use C# because it's both modern and simple, and its functionalities support the best practices for object-oriented design and programming. C# is a powerful, versatile programming language that can be used to develop a variety of applications using the basic console, windows, intranet/Internet, web services and mobile applications as well as a component and embedded systems development approach. C# can also be used to develop systems software like operating systems, compilers/interpreters, device drivers, database management systems, utilities, software development tools, etc. C# was created by Microsoft Corporation's .NET research division and is a case-sensitive language (meaning that the variable name '*firstName*' is different from '*firstname*').

THE .NET FRAMEWORK

The .NET Framework is a systems software product developed by Microsoft Corporation's .NET research division. It provides an environment that can support and manage pure object-oriented application systems development for several object-oriented programming languages, including C#. In order to program with and understand the C# programming language, you must understand the .NET Framework structure. C# is one of several programming languages targeted for the .NET Framework, thus all C# applications are best suited for development in the .NET Framework and Microsoft Visual Studio environments (Visual Studio is explained later in this chapter).

The .NET Framework has thousands of predefined functions/methods in classes that are available to developers. These classes are grouped into '***Namespaces***'. These 'Namespaces' contain a group of user-defined data types called '***classes***'. These 'classes' contain *'public'* members that provide further functionalities to support and promote the maximum use of the RAD (rapid application development) programming paradigm. With the .NET Framework Class Library, you can create any kind of real-life application system with minimal coding effort. It gives you access to almost any function that you could need to write your application. All you have to do is include the functionalities in your application (C# uses the identifier *'using'* to include 'namespace' functionalities in a program). To learn more about the .NET Framework Class Library functionalities, refer to the .NET Framework documentation on your computer or go to Microsoft's website and search for the .NET Framework Class Library.

The .NET Framework, in collaboration with the Visual Studio Development Tool, is a complete platform for object-oriented application systems development. Visual Studio provides an extremely rich environment for C# application development. All of the programming examples in this book are based on C# projects in the Visual Studio Software Development Environment using the services of the .NET Framework Class Library.

UNDERSTANDING C# .NET PROGRAMMING LANGUAGE BASICS

C# is a comprehensive object-oriented programming language, and as such, a typical C# application will be made up of one or more *'classes'*. C# supports the principle of object reusability in object-oriented design and programming. The word 'class' is a keyword identifier used in C# to declare one of its user-defined data types. 'Class' is a container that encapsulates, or hides, the implementation and behaviors of its members. C# has several access levels for functions that want to use services from another class. All data type declarations, fields, properties, functions, events, etc., are contained in a *'class'*. When programming with C#, all code is executed in a class. The following are a few very simple, but complete, C# programs in a Visual Studio Development Environment:

Basic C# Console Program in Visual Studio	Basic C# Windows Program in Visual Studio
```using System; namespace ConsoleApp { class MyConsoleProgram { static void Main (string[ ] args) { // declare all variables here string myMsg = "Console APP and "; string myName = "my name is John"; // display the message on the console Console.WriteLine(myMsg + myName); } } }```	```using System.Windows.Forms; namespace WindowsApp { public partial class WinOne : Form { public WinOne () { InitializeComponent (); } private void WinOne_Load(object sender, EventArgs e) { // declare all variables here string myMsg = "Windows App and "; string myName = "my name is John"; // display the message in windows MessageBox.Show(myMsg + myName); } } }```

The word **'using'** is what the C# compiler uses to include functionalities from the predefined *'classes'* so that those functions can be used in your *'class'* (program). For instance, the **'Console.WriteLine ()'** function displays a message to the user in a console application and is a function/method in the **System** namespace. The **'MessageBox.Show ()'** function, which displays information to the user in a Windows application, is in the **System.Windows.Forms** namespace. When developing application in a Visual Studio environment, the C# compiler is so smart that it will globally analyze the project type and automatically resolve dependencies from other classes in the .NET Framework Class Library to help the programmer. The C# compiler is smart enough to know what the functional dependencies from the .NET Framework Class Library are, in order to make them available to console, windows, intranet/internet, web service, or mobile projects. Your actual program is everything inside the word *'class'* between the '{' and '}' characters.

The word **'namespace'** is a unique project name. It contains one or more classes in a single project. It's like a package in Java that groups all related functionalities together and encapsulates them from other projects. When you use Visual Studio to develop an application, your project name will become your namespace name. For instance, in the previous two applications, **'ConsoleApp'** is the project name for the Console application and **'WindowsApp'** is the project name for the Windows application.

C# BUILT-IN PRIMITIVE DATA TYPES

The following section explains some of the most common built-in primitive data types that are part of the C# programming language with practical examples.

'BOOL' DATA TYPE

The 'bool' data type is used to declare a variable identifier to store logical values of either *'true'* or *'false'*. The default value is 'false'. The following example demonstrates how to use the 'bool' data type in a windows application:

```
using System.Windows.Forms;    // MessageBox.Show is in this namespace
public class BoolDataType
{
    public BoolDataType()   // constructor method - same name as the class
    {
        // declare variables to use in this program
        bool verifyGender = false;
        string genderType = " ";
        // get data entry from the user to check for gender
        if (genderType == "female")
        {
            verifyGender = true;
            MessageBox.Show ("Hi Reader, I noticed you are a FEMALE");
        }
        else
            MessageBox.Show ("Hi Reader, I noticed you are a MALE");
    }
} /* end of BoolDataType class */
```

'BYTE' DATA TYPE

This data type is used to declare and define a byte variable identifier. It stores numbers from 0 to 255. The default value is 0. The following example demonstrates how to use the 'byte' data type in application:

```
public class ByteDataType
{
    public ByteDataType()   // constructor method – same name as the class
    {
        byte smallInteger = 8;    // byte variable declared and initialized
        const byte maxByteInCsharP = 255;   // maximum byte value in C#
    }
} /* end of ByteDataType class */
```

'CHAR' DATA TYPE

The 'char' data type is used to declare and define a character variable identifier. It stores all single characters (e.g., "A" or "a", or special characters like "#", "@", "$", etc.). The following example demonstrates how to use the 'char' data type in a console application:

```
using System;
public class CharDataType
{
    public CharDataType()  // constructor method – same name as the class
    {
        // declare a char variable myChar and initialize it to spaces
        char myChar = ' ';
        // now assign the dollar sign to myChar variable
        myChar  = '$';
        /* display the content of myChar variable on the console */
        Console.WriteLine ("My character is " + myChar);
    }
} /* end of CharDataType class */
```

This is the result of running the above program.

```
My character is  $
```

'DECIMAL' DATA TYPE

The 'decimal' data type is used to declare and define a variable identifier to store money. It isn't subject to rounding. It's usually used for financial calculations. The following example demonstrates how to use the 'decimal' data type in a console application:

```
using System;      // Console.WriteLine method is in this namespace
public class DecimalDataType
{
    public DecimalDataType()    // the constructor  - same name as the class
    {
        // declare and initialize decimal variables
        decimal myAccountBalance = 0.00m, myTodayWithdraw   = 0.00m;
        // get my account balance from the bank database
        myAccountBalance   = 20000.00;
        // get the amount to withdraw from account using account number
        myTodayWithdraw   = 4000.00;
        // calculate my current account balance after withdrawal
        myAccountBalance = (myAccountBalance -  myTodayWithdraw);
        /* display the content of myAccountBalance on the console */
        Console.WriteLine ("My Balance is " + "$" + myAccountBalance);
    }
}   /* end of DecimalDataType class   */
```

The result of the above program would be as follows.

My Balance is $16000.00

'INT' DATA TYPE

This is used to declare and define an integer variable identifier. The content of a variable defined as 'int' can store integer values between -2147483648 and 2147483647 (32 bits). The following example demonstrates how to use the 'int' data type in a console application:

```
using System;
public class IntDataType
{
    public IntDataType()   // constructor method - same name as the class
    {
        // declare and initialize int data type variables
        int intOne = 0, intTwo = 0, myResult = 0;
        // assign values to intOne and intTwo integer variables
        intOne = 4800, intTwo = 200;
        // add intOne and intTwo and place the result in the myResult variable
        myResult   = (intOne + intTwo);
        /* display the content of myResult variable on the console */
        Console.WriteLine ("My Integer addition result is " + myResult);
    }
}   // end of IntDataType class
```

This is the result of running the above program.

My Integer addition result is 5000

'LONG' DATA TYPE

You use the 'long' data type to declare and define a variable that stores integer values between -9223372036854775808 and 9223372036854775807 (64 bits). Normally you won't bother yourself with these large numbers, but this will help you deal with larger numbers that cannot be handled by the 'int' data type. The following example shows how the 'long data type is declared and initialized in application:

```
public class LongDataType
{
    public LongDataType()  // constructor method — same name as the class
    {
        long anyIntegerForLongDataType = 200L;
        long myLargeIntegerValue = 2147483649;
        const long maxLongDataType = 9223372036854775807;
    }
} /* end of LongDataType class */
```

'FLOAT' DATA TYPE

The 'float' data type is used to declare and define a variable identifier to store real/decimal numbers with up to 7 – 9 significant numbers/digits (32 bits). Example as follows:

```
float myFloat = 0.0f;            // initialize myFloat variable with zero value
myFloat = 475.804657829f;        // assign a value to 'my'Float'
```

'DOUBLE' DATA TYPE

The 'double' data type is used to declare and define a variable identifier that can store long real/decimal numbers up to 15 – 16 significant/digits (64 bits). You use this data type for real numbers that cannot be handled by the *float* data type. Example as follows:

```
double myDouble = 0.0;                    // initialize myDouble variable with zero
double myDouble = 475.8975836252642;      // assign a value to 'myDouble'
```

'STRING' DATA TYPE

The 'string' data type is used to declare and define variable identifier that stores a 'string' (a sequence of characters like a text message). It's actually a reference or a pointer direction for a string object where the value of the string starts in the memory. The following example demonstrates how to use the 'string' data type in a console application:

```
public class StringDataType
{
    public StringDataType()   // constructor - same name as the class
    {
        // declare and initialize the string variables
        string userPswd = " ", userName = " ", saluTation = " ";
        string firstName = " ", middleName = " ", lastName = " ", fullName = " ";
        // get user info from the database using the userName variable
        firstName  = "Mary", middleName = "Rose, lastName = "Murphy";
        saluTation = "Ms";
        // build the full name to display on the command line
        fullName = (saluTation + ".  " + firstName + " " + middleName + " " + lastName);
        /* now display the content of fullName on the console */
        System.Console.WriteLine ("My Name is " + fullName);
    }
}   //   end of StringDataType class
```

When this program is run the results are as follows.

My Name is Ms. Rose Mary Murphy

USING ARRAYS IN C#

As explained in chapter 2 under "Programming Language Characteristics," an array is a collection of variables that belong to the same data type with a fixed length (meaning that the number of memory locations the programmer is requesting is fixed). Each item in the group is called an element of the array and is accessed using an integer index. The following examples show how arrays are declared and used in C#:

```
int [ ] studentsAges;      // integer array declaration without initialization
studentsAges = { 23, 22, 19, 20, 21 }     // now initialized with five students ages
float [ ] studentsGPA = { 4.0, 3.5, 3.2, 3.0 }      // float array declaration with initialization
string [ ] studentNames; // string array declaration without initialization
studentNames = { "Fred Todd", "Jim Coban", "Joan Bath" } // now initialized with 3 items
```

In C#, the items in an array are accessed through an index with 0 referring to the first item. That means the first element in the array in the above integer, float, and string arrays declaration, is accessed as follows:

```
int firstYearStudentAge = studentsAges [0];          // get the first age in the array
float firstYearStudentGPA = studentsGPA [3];         // get the fourth GPA in the array
string firstYearStudentName = studentNames [1];      // get the second name in the array
```

The content of the above integer variable *'firstYearStudentAge'* will be '**23**'. The content of the float variable *'firstYearStudentGPA'* will be '**3.0**' and the content of the above string variable *'firstYearStudentName'* will be '**Jim Coban**'.

As usual, the .NET Framework Class Library has an array class in the '**System**' namespace with properties and methods to manage arrays to save the programmer the work of writing complex algorithms to handle an array. For instance, the following example provides the total number of items in the *'studentNames'* array:

```
int totalNames = studentNames.Length;    // value in the variable totalNames will be 3
```

There are also methods in the array class to clear, reverse, and sort the array. The following examples show how you can use these methods:

```
Array.Clear (studentNames);            // delete all items from the studentNames array
Array.Sort (studentNames);             // sort the items in the studentNames array
Array.Reverse (studentNames);          // reverse the items in the studentNames
```

USING COLLECTIONS IN C#

'Collections' in C# are extremely important because almost every application you develop, you will use one or more 'Collections'. Collections represent a group of objects with one identifier/name. These objects are reusable collection of data structures. The .NET Framework Class Library has some classes in '**System.Collections.Generic**' namespace with methods that support the declaration and usage of 'data structures/collections' like ArrayList, List, Queue, Stack etc. Unlike the 'Array', other data structures like 'List', store data types (objects) belonging to the same data type but without fixed length (i.e., 'List' is a type-safety data structure). The following example demonstrates how to declare and use 'the 'List' data structure/collection:

```
using System.Data.SqlClient;           // Reader.read method is in this namespace
using System.Collections.Generic;      // the List<T> data structure is in this namespace
public class listCollectionSample
{
    // declare and initialize integer variable called 'totalStudents'
    int totalStudents = 0;
    string studentFullName = " ";
    /* declare a variable call 'studentNames' as 'List' data type */
    List<string> studentNames = new List<string> ();
    public listCollectionSample ()   // constructor - same name as the class
    {
```

```
        studentNames.Clear ();     // initialize the list to null/spaces
        while (Reader.read)      //  reading the database
        {
          studentFullName = Database.StudentFullName;
          studentNames.Add (studentFullName);     // load the students list
          totalSudents = (totalStudents + 1);        // increase total students by 1
        }
        Console.WriteLine ("Total number of first year students is " + totalStudents);
    }
} // end of listCollectionSample class
```

The above example demonstrates that you have declared a *'List'* variable known as *'studentNames'* to be used to load student names from a database. The most important part in the above program example is how the *'List'* is declared and the methods *'Clear'* and *'Add'* used to initialize and load the *'studentNames'* to the list respectively.

C# USER-DEFINED DATA TYPES

As explained in chapter 2, user-defined data types are the data types that the programmer can create. Some of the types that you can create in the C# programming language include the following:

Data Type	Purpose
Class	Defines a new data type and operations that interact with the type. *'Class'* actually originates from *'structure'* and gives it more functionalities and capabilities.
Structure	Creates a composite data type using a group of primitive data types with one identifier. Allows limited functions to operate on the primitive data types.
Exception	Assists the programmer in controlling and exposing all errors in a meaningful way and in understanding error messages for the programmer/user during execution without shutting down an application due to a fatal error.
Enumeration	Defines a range of named values for a specific data type.

THE 'CLASS' USER-DEFINED DATA TYPE DECLARATION

The identifier (name) *'class'* in C# is used by the programmer to declare a user-defined data type. A typical class syntax declaration is as follows:

```
public class myFirstClass
{
        /// list of all the members in myFirstClass
        /* no client can contact my member unless through me */
        // come get my member only if you see the word 'public'
        // if you are my child you can use all my 'protected' and 'public' members
        /* I also have the option to be abstract, sealed and static */
} // end of myFirstClass class
```

CLASS MEMBERS

'Class' contains members that expose functionalities and maintain an instance of the *'class'* (usually called an object) in the correct state. This section describes most of the members in a C# *'class'* container.

'FIELD' CLASS MEMBER

This is the identifier you use to request a memory location to store a variable data type. Example as follows:

```
using System;
public class fieldSamplesInAClass
{
    int studentAge = 0;              //  integer field declaration in a class
    string studentName = " ";        //  string field declaration in a class
    char currencySign = ' ';         // character field declaration in a class
}    // end of fieldSamplesInAClass class
```

The declared variable names studentAge, studentName and currencySign are all 'fields'.

'CONSTANT' CLASS MEMBER

This is the identifier for declaring a data type with a value that never changes during the life time of a program execution. Example as follows:

```
public class constantSamplesInAClass
{
    const int studentAge = 23;            // integer constant field declaration
    const float maxAdmitGPA =  4.0;       // float constant field declaration
    const char usCurrencySign = '$';      // character constant declaration
}    // end of constantSamplesInAClass class
```

'PROPERTY' CLASS MEMBER

Property is an attribute (field) of a class that describes the characteristics of that class. But unlike a field, which has a fixed length set by the language designer (and which the compiler   abides), property can be managed and controlled by the programmer. Property is usually referred to as *'smart field'*. Example as follows:

```
public class propertySamplesInAClass ()
{
    private string user-name = " ";
    public string User-Name
    {
        get { return user-name; }
        set { user-name = value; }
    }
    private string user-pswd = " ";
    public string User-Pswd
    {
        get { return user-pswd; }
        set { user-pswd = value; }
    }
}    // end of propertySamplesInAClass class
```

The following is how to access *'User-Name'* and *'User-Pswd'* properties in the above *'propertySamplesInAClass'* class in application:

```
propertySamplesInAClass userProfile = new propertySamplesInAClass ();
userProfile.User-Name = "tomBow";          // set user name
userProfile.User-Pswd = "nyawas101";       // set user password
string theUser = userProfile.User-Name;    // get the content of user name
```

'CONSTRUCTOR' CLASS MEMBER

This is a function used by clients to create an instance of a class (e.g., to request memory to perform functions using the blueprint of a class). The constructor function always has the same name as the class and they never return a value, even though they have the option to accept parameters from callers. There can be more than one constructor in a class but they're identified by the levels of parameters. The following example shows how two "constructor" functions/methods are declared in a class:

```
public class constructorSamplesInAClass
{
```

```
    public constructorSamplesInAClass ()
    {
/* I'm a constructor method, use me to create an instance of this class — my name is always
the same as my class container. I'm the one known as 'object' when you call me. I don't need
any parameter(s) — just call me so that you can use this class. Initialize all components in
your project here */
    }
    public constructorSamplesInAClass (string userName)
    {
/* I'm also a constructor method, use me to create an instance of this class — my name is always
the same as my class container. I'm the one known as 'object' when you call me. I need your
userName before you can use my services. Initialize all components in your project here */
    }
} // end of constructorSamplesInAClass class
```

'METHOD' CLASS MEMBER

C# calls a function "method". This follows the same concept as a function, like f(x), in algebra in basic mathematics that performs specific tasks for a class or an instance of a class (e.g., object). C# also allows for overloaded methods (this means that several methods can have the same name in the same class, as long as they have different lists of parameters, usually referred to as the method signature). Here we can see an example of this:

```
using System;
public class methodSamplesInAClass
{
    public methodSamplesInAClass ()   // constructor method — same name as class
    {
        // initialize project components here (i.e all project declared variables)
    }
 /* I'm a method and my name is 'addTwoNumbers'. Call me without parameters because
I don't need it, but make sure variables 'numOne' and 'numTwo' have values and I will
display the result on the console — I can only be used in this class because I'm not public */
    void addTwoNumbers ()
    {
        int total = (numOne + numTwo);
        System.Console.WriteLine (total);
    }
 /* I'm also 'addTwoNumbers' method but call me with parameters because I need them to get
you the results you want, but make sure variables 'numOne' and 'numTwo' have values before
you call me else you won't get the result you are looking for. I can only be used in this class
*/
    int addTwoNumbers (int numOne, int numTwo)
```

```
    {
        int total = (numOne + numTwo);
        return total;
    }
} // end of methodSamplesInAClass class
```

'EVENT' CLASS MEMBER

Event is a special function (method) used to provide notifications during run time (during program execution). This is extremely useful in Windows, intranet/Internet, and mobile applications.

```
using System.Windows.Forms;
public class eventSamplesInAClass ()
{
    // I'm a button object. Click me and I will react. I'm an event handler
    private void submit_Click(object sender, EventArgs e)
    {
        MessageBox.Show ("Hi there, you just Clicked me");
    }
    // I'm a button object control. Place the mouse on me and I will react
    private void submit_MouseHover(object sender, EventArgs e)
    {
        MessageBox.Show ("Hi there, the mouse is hovering over me");
    }
} // end of eventSamplesInAClass class
```

CLASS ACCESSIBILITY

'Class' and its members have the option to decide which client can have access to their functionalities (behavior). The following section describes the basic C# class member access level privileges.

'PUBLIC' ACCESS LEVEL

Clients can access any public member in a 'class'. Example as follows:

```
public class publicAccess
{
    public const double mathPie = 3.14159;   // call and use me anywhere
    public publicAccess ()     // constructor – same name as the class
    {
        // initialize all application components here
    }
    /* Example of a public method to use to withdraw money from a bank */
```

```
    public decimal WithdrawMoney (string actNumber, decimal amount)
    {
        // logic to check for account balance and withdraw amount here
    }
} // end of publicAccess  class
```

'PROTECTED' ACCESS LEVEL

Only this 'class' and its children (sub-classes that inherit the parent class) have access to 'protected' members. Example as follows:

```
public class protectedAccess
{
/* Math pie constant value can be accessed by only inherited class in this application. Only me and my children can use me */
    protected const double mathPie = 3.14159;
    public protectedAccess ()
    {
/* I'm   a constructor method for this class, and my name is the same as my class. Use me to create an instance of this class to initialize an object in memory */
    }
/* Example of a protected method to be used to withdraw money from bank account */
    protected decimal WithdrawMoney(string actNumber, decimal amount)
    {
        // operations to check for account balance and withdraw amount
    }
} // end of protectedAccess class
```

'PRIVATE' ACCESS LEVEL

Private members in a class can only be accessed by the class itself. Example as follows:

```
using System.Windows.Forms;
public class privateAccess
{
/* declare and initialize variables first name, middle name and last name to be used in this class only */
    private string fName = "John ", mName = "Dim ", lName = "Chow"
    public privateAccess ()
    {
/* I'm a constructor method for this class, and my name is the same as my class.Use me to create an instance of this class to initialize an object in memory so that you can use my functionalities and capabilities */
    }
    // Example of a private method to be used to create a full name
```

```
    private void CreateFullName ()
    {
        string fullName = (fName  + ", " +  mName + " " + lName);
        /* display full name to the user in a windows application */
        MessageBox.Show ("Hi, my name is   " + fullName);
    }
} // end of privateAccess class
```

The following is the outcome when the method 'CreateFullName' is called:

Hi, my name is John, Dim Chow

Note that if you don't specifically state a class member accessibility level in your program, the compiler will use the default level which is 'private' (i.e., no other class members, or clients, in your application domain can access your class members). The following is an example of the syntax '*class*' declaration for a basic banking application system where all branch bank transactions are managed at the head office:

```
using System;
public class BankHeadOfficeTransactions
{
    private string verificationResult = " ", branch-ID = " ";    // use me only in this class
    private bool phoneOrTextMsg = false;  //  me too – use me only in this class
    public BankHeadOfficeTransactions ()    // the constructor method
    {
        initializeComponents ();    // this method initializes all variables in this app
    }
    public BankHeadOfficeTransactions (string yourBranchID)
    {
        // I'm also a constructor, but call me with your bank branch ID
        branch-ID =  yourBranchID;
        startUpMethod ();     // calling the private startUpMethod method/function
    }
    private void startUpMethod ()
    {
        // logic to verify branch-ID from the bank database
    }
    protected string getBankCurrentName ()
    {
        // logic to retrieve bank name from the bank database
    }
    public string openAccount (decimal amountToStartOpeningAccount)
    {
```

```
        // invoke a form to collect information about the potential consumer
    }
    public string closeAccount (string accountNumber)
    {
        // delete customer from customer database using accountNumber
    }
    public decimal getAccountBalance (string accountNumber)
    {
        // operation to return the balance to the caller here
    }
    public decimal withdrawMoney (string accountNumber, decimal amount)
    {
        // operation to return the amount withdrawn to the caller here
    }
} // end of BankHeadOfficeTransactions class
```

The above class can have other class members like 'fields', 'constants', 'properties', and additional 'methods' like 'verifyAccountNumber', 'transferMoney', etc. In the next section, we can see how to create and use an instance of the above 'BankHeadOfficeTransactions' class.

CLASS INSTANCES

'**Class**' is a data type just like 'int' is a data type. So, in order to use a class to access its members, you have to declare a variable of that class (in C# a class instance declaration is known as an 'object'). To create an instance of a class, use the keyword '**new**' and to access the public members of the class, add the dot notation (.) and specify the name of the member. The following 'CustomerFirst' class shows how to declare a variable type from the above 'BankHeadOfficeTransactions' class and access its public member 'openAccount' method:

```
using System.Windows.Forms;
public class CustomerFirst
{
// declare a variable called thisBranch to be of a type BankHeadOfficeTransactions class
    BankHeadOfficeTransactions thisBranch = new BankHeadOfficeTransactions ();
    public CustomerFirst ()   // constructor - call me to create instance of this class
    {
        /* invoke a method that verifies id and background check */
        if ((government-issued-Id == true) & (credit-background == ok))
        {
                decimal myMoney = 4800.00;    // customer money to open account
```

```
            string textMsg = thisBranch.openAccount (myMoney);
            MessageBox.Show ("Hi, Congratulations - " + textMsg);
        }
    }
} // end of CustomerFirst class
```

CLASS AND INHERITANCE

In C# every data type implicitly inherits a root class known as '*object*' class and, as such, has access to all '*public*' and '*protected*' members of the 'object' class. For instance, there's a method in the 'object' class called '***ToString ()***' that translates the content of a variable of any data type to the 'string' data type. The C# language therefore allows the programmer to create a sub-class (a child class) that inherits parent class functionalities. A sub-class automatically inherits all '*protected*' and '*public*' members of the parent class. C# uses the colon character (' : ') as a symbol for a child class to inherit a parent class. The following example shows how a child class called '*thisBranchUniqueOperations*' is declared to inherit a parent class called '*BankHeadOfficeTransactions*' so that the child can have access to all the parent public and protected members:

```
public class thisBranchUniqueOperations : BankHeadOfficeTransactions
{
        // all 'thisBranchUniqueOperations' class members here
}
```

MANAGING CLASSES

The C# language allows the programmer to manage and control classes for client usage in an application. The following section describes the class management type usage with declaration examples:

'ABSTRACT' CLASS

Abstract classes can't be instantiated, but can be inherited. These are good to use for a parent (base) class where common functionalities are listed, but implemented by children classes. The declaration is made as follows:

```
public abstract class allVehiclesCommonFunctionalities
{
/* only common vehicles methods signature here. My children will create varied detailed
implementation of my methods - no instances */
}
```

'SEALED' CLASS

Sealed classes can be instantiated, but can't be inherited. If you don't want any child classes because you want all method implementations in a parent (base) class, then you mark your class as sealed; and the compiler will make sure that no child class inherits that base class. The declaration is made as follows:

```
public sealed class mathAndPhysicsFormulaClass
{
    public mathAndPhysicsFormulaClass () // constructor method
    {
        initializeComponents ();    // initialize all variables in this app
    }
    // implement all my member methods here – no inheritance
}
```

'STATIC' CLASS

Static classes allow other classes in the application to use their members directly without creating an instance variable of the class. All members in a static class must use the word 'static' as part of their declaration. The following is an example of a static class declaration:

```
using System.Windows.Forms;
public static class propertiesAndMessages
{
    public static string compName = "ABC Ltd.";
    private static string username = " ", password = " ";
    public static string UserName
    {
        get { return username; }
        set { username = value; }
    }
    public static string PassWord
    {
        get { return password; }
        set { password = value; }
    }
    public static void displayMessage (string theMsg)
    {
        MessageBox.Show (theMsg);
    }
} // end of propertiesAndMessages class
```

The following shows how to access the 'compName' field, 'UserName' and 'PassWord' properties and the 'displayMessage' method in the following 'manageUserProfile' class (remember that you don't need to create an instance variable for the type *propertiesAndMessages* class because it's static):

```
using System.Windows.Forms;
public class manageUserProfile
{
    string myMsg = "Hi, I'm going to use your public members.";
    string username = " ", pswd = " ";
    public manageUserProfile ()    // constructor method
    {
        MessageBox.Show (propertiesAndMessages.compName);
        propertiesAndMessages.displayMessage (myMsg)
        setUserProfile ();    // update user profile info
        getUserProfile ();    // retrieve user profile info
    {
    private void setUserProfile ()   // update user profile info method
    {
        username = "kalala99 ", pswd = "alotey101";
        propertiesAndMessages.UserName = username;
        propertiesAndMessages.PassWord = pswd;
    }
    private void getUserProfile ()   // retrieve user profile info method
    {
        username = propertiesAndMessages.UserName;
        pswd = propertiesAndMessages.PassWord;
    }
} // end of manageUserProfile class
```

MANAGING METHODS

As explained earlier in chapter 2, a function is one of the most important features in any programming language. An application is nothing but one or more functions working together by exchanging data and messages through parameter passing among the functions. As a potential computer programmer, the first thing to understand about any programming language is how a function is declared and used in a program. Functions receive parameters, declare and use data types, have conditional and logical operations, call other functions in their scope to achieve a specific task. Some functions receive parameter(s) and return values, while others receive parameter(s), but don't return values. Other functions don't receive parameters and don't return values to the function caller. In the C# programming language, a function is known as a *'method'* and a method is one of the members in a class.

To develop a C# application system, you must thoroughly understand the structure, purpose, usage, and characteristics of a method. In C#, all methods are declared in a class and all code execution happens in methods within a class. The following examples show how a method is declared in the C# programming language. Assume that all of these examples are declared in the following *'ManageMethods'* class:

```
using System;
using System.Windows.Forms;
public class ManageMethods
{
    public ManageMethods ();            // the constructor of this class
    {
        initializeComponents ();        // initialize all declared variables
    }
    // place all the methods example bellow here
} // end of ManageMethods class
```

The following example declares a private method called *'connect-Database'* in the above *'ManageMethods'* class that doesn't receive parameter(s) and doesn't return any value. The word 'private' means that this method can be called only within the above *'ManageMethods'* class. The word 'void' means this method doesn't return any value to the caller and the identifier *'connect-Database'* is the name of the method. The empty brackets '**()**' mean that this method doesn't receive parameter(s) and the characters '**{**' and '**}**' is the beginning and end respectively of the method, just like they are used to contain class scope (members).

```
private void connect-Database ()
{
// scope of this method - place the operation to connect database here
}
```

The following is how you call (use) the above method in the above 'ManageMethods' class:

```
connect-Database ();  // i.e. calling the above connect-Database method
```

The following example declares a public method called *'displayMessage'* in the above

'*ManageMethods*' class that receives one string parameter known as '*theMsg*', but doesn't return any value. The method then uses the content of '*theMsg*' to display a message in a Windows application by calling the '*MessageBox.Show*' method with the '*theMsg*' parameter to display the actual message.

```
public void displayMessage (string theMsg)
{
    MessageBox.Show (theMsg);
}
```

The following example declares a public method called '*connect-Database*' in the above '*ManageMethods*' class that receives one parameter, and returns a value. The word 'public' means this method can be called (used) by all classes in this application. The word 'string' means this method returns a 'string' data type value. The word 'return' is a keyword used to exit the function.

```
public string connect-Database (string userName)
{
    string results = "not successful";   // declare string variable 'results' and initialize it
    if (databaseConnection is successful)
    {
        results = "is successful";
    }
    return results;
}
```

The following '*connectDatabaseAndDisplayMessage*' private method shows how you use the above '*displayMessage*' and '*connect-Database*' methods within the '*ManageMethods*' class:

```
private void connectDatabaseAndDisplayMessage ()
{
    string operationResult = connect-Database (); // calling the connect-Database method
    displayMessage ("Database Connection status: " + operationResult);
}
```

Note that if you're calling the '*displayMessage*' and '*connect-Database*' methods from a different class, then you have to declare a variable from the 'ManageMethods' data type before you can use it. The following '*MyDbaseMsgs*' class uses the services of '*ManageMethods*' class:

```
using System;
public class MyDbaseMsgs
{
    string pswd = "sysadmin";
    ManageMethods myMethod = new ManageMethods ();
    string operationResult = myMethod.connect-Database (pswd);
    myMethod.displayMessage ("Database Connection status: " + operationResult);
}
```

The following example declares a public method called *createFullName* in the above *ManageMethods* class that receives three 'string' variable parameters known as *firstName*, *middleName*, and *lastName*, and return a value in 'fullName' variable to the function caller. The method declares a string variable known as *fullName* and uses its content as the return value to leave the method.

```
public string createFullName (string firstName, string middleName, string lastName)
{
    string fullName = " ";       // declare string data type variable 'fullName'
    if (middleName != " ")
    {
        fullName = (firstName + " " + middleName + " " + lastName);
    else
        fullName = (firstName + " " + lastName);
    }
    return fullName;
}
```

The following example shows how you use the above *createFullName* method within the *ManageMethods* class:

```
private UsingCreateFullNameMethodInThisClass ()
{
    string fName = "James", mName = "Anthony", lName = "Simpson", fullName = " ";
    fullName = createFullName (fName, mName, lName);
    MessageBox.Show ("The employee full name is " + fullName);
}
```

To use the *createFullName* method in another class, you have to create an instance of the *ManageMethods* class because *ManageMethods* class is not declared as 'static'. The following example shows how you use the *createFullName* method in a different class in your application:

```
using System;
public class UsingManageMethodsClass
{
    public UsingManageMethodsClass ();    // the constructor of this class
    {
        initializeComponents ();    // initialize all declared variables
    }
    private usingManageMethodsServices ()
    {
        ManageMethods myMethod = new ManageMethods ();
        string fName = "John", mName = "Tom", lName = "Doe", fullName = " ";
        fullName = myMethod.createFullName (fName, mName, lName);
        myMethod.displayMessage ("The employee full name is " + fullName);
    }
// rest of class members here
} // end of UsingManageMethodsClass class
```

VIRTUAL METHOD

Good object-oriented programming encourages the practice of the concept of inheritance where a child class inherits the parent class functionalities. In C# the child class (derived class) automatically inherits all the 'protected' and 'public' members of the parent class. C# allows the child class to override the operations of its parent class method by decorating that method with the word 'virtual'. The following example demonstrates how to declare a 'virtual' method in a base (parent) class to be overridden by child classes:

```
using System.Windows.Forms;    // need it for MessageBox.Show method
public class ParentBaseClass
{
    public ParentBaseClass ();    // the constructor of this class
    {
        initializeComponents ();         // initialize all declared variables
    }
    public virtual void displayMessage (string theMsg)
    {
        MessageBox.Show (theMsg);
    }
} // end of ParentBaseClass class
```

OVERRIDDEN METHOD

Every 'public' or 'protected' method in a base class that is decorated with the word 'virtual' can be overridden by all derived classes (sub-classes). For a derived class to override a method in the base class to provide a different implementation for that method you must decorate that method in the sub-class with the word *'override'*. The following example demonstrates how the *'displayMessage'* method in the above *'ParentBaseClass'* can be overridden and implemented differently in two children classes:

```
using System.Windows.Forms;              // need it for MessageBox.Show method
public class ChildClassOne : ParentBaseClass    // ChildClass inherits ParentBaseClass
{
    public ChildClassOne ();            // the constructor of this class
    {
        initializeComponents ();        // initialize all declared variables
    }
    public override void displayMessage (string theMsg)
    {
        MessageBox.Show (theMsg, CompanyClass.Name);
    }
} // end of ChildClassOne class
using System.Windows.Forms;          // need it for MessageBox.Show method
public class ChildClassTwo : ParentBaseClass    // ChildClass inherits ParentBaseClass
{
    public ChildClassTwo ();              // the constructor of this class
    {
        initializeComponents ();        // initialize all declared variables
    }
    public override void displayMessage (string theMsg)
    {
        MessageBox.Show (theMsg, CompClass.Name, MessageBoxButtons.OK);
    }
} // end of ChildClassTwo class
```

In the above examples, the 'displayMessage' methods in the derived classes 'ChildClassOne' and 'ChildClassTwo' have overridden the 'ParentBaseClass' 'displayMessage' method with different implementation. Instead of calling the popular windows application method 'MessageBox.Show' (which is in the namespace 'System.Windows.Forms') with one parameter, the 'ChildClassOne' implements the method differently by calling MessageBox.Show method with two parameters. The second argument ('CompanyClass') is a static class in your application which has a public static field called 'Name' or a public static property called 'Name' which contains the name of a company name to be displayed as part of the message. The 'ChildClassTwo' on the other hand implements the method differently by calling MessageBox.Show method with three parameters. The third parameter uses the 'OK' property in MessageBoxButtons enumeration list.

OVERLOADED METHOD

The C# programming language has a feature that implements the concept of overloaded functions/methods. This feature allows methods in the same class to have the same name, but different method signatures (meaning a method with a different number of parameters). The following static class example shows how to declare overloaded methods in the same class:

```
using System.Windows.Forms;        // need it for MessageBox.Show method
public static class MessagesClass   // no need to create a class instance
{
    // the following 'displayMessage' method does not expect any parameter
    public static void displayMessage ()
    {
        MessageBox.Show ("Hi there, Welcome to Computer Programming");
    }
    // the following 'displayMessage' method expects one parameter
    public static void displayMessage (string theMsg)
    {
        MessageBox.Show (theMsg);
    }
    // the following 'displayMessage' method expects two parameters
    public static void displayMessage (string theMsg, string companyName)
    {
        MessageBox.Show (theMsg, companyName);
    }
} // end of MessagesClass class
```

The C# compiler is smart enough to resolve a call to the three overloaded methods. The following 'UsingMessagesClassServices' class example demonstrates how you call (use) the three methods in the above static 'MessagesClass' class in your application:

```
using System;
public class UsingMessagesClassServices
{
    string aMsg = "Hi there, Welcome to Computer Programming";
    string compName = "AsioTechnologies";
    public UsingMessagesClassServices    // constructor method
    {
        initializeComponents ();  // initialize all declared variables in this app
        useMessagesClass ();    // call this private method in this class
    }
    private void useMessagesClass ()
```

```
    {
        MessagesClass.displayMessage ();    // call displayMessage with no parameter
        MessagesClass.displayMessage (aMsg);          // call with one parameter
        MessagesClass.displayMessage (aMsg, compName);    // call with two parameters
    }
} // end of UsingMessagesClassServices class
```

STRUCTURE USER-DEFINED DATA TYPE DECLARATION

Structure is another very important user-defined data type. In C# it's a group of primi-tive data types and methods to work on those types. Normally, if you don't need a class with several members, such as properties, several methods, or events, it's good program-ming practice to use the 'structure' user-defined data type. As explained in chapter 2, structures live on the *'stack'* instead of the *'heap'*. Structure has a default constructor, but you can overload the constructor with at least one parameter. The following is the declaration format for the 'structure' user-defined data type:

```
struct   structureName
{
// structure members
}
```

The following example declares and defines a 'structure' called *'fullNameMaker'* with three public fields, one private field and one method:

```
public struct fullNameMaker
{
    public string firstName = " ", middleName = " ", lastName = " ";
    private string fullName = " ";
    public string organizeFullName ()
    {
        if (middleName != " ")
        {
            fullName = (firstName +  " " + middleName + " " + lastName);
        }
        else
        {
            fullName = (firstName +   " " + lastName);
        }
        return fullName;
    } // end of  organizeFullName method
} // end of fullNameMaker structure
```

To use 'structure', you have to create an instance just like class by using the **'new'** keyword, and to use structure members, you use the dot notation (**.**). The following example shows how you use the *'fullNameMaker'* structure in an *'employeeBenefit'* class in your application:

```
using System.Data.SqlClient;    // Reader.read method is this namespace
public class employeeBenefit
{
    private string employeeFullName = " ";  // variable to use in this class only
    List<employees> employeeFullNameList = new List<employees> ();
    fullNameMaker fullName = new fullNameMaker(); // fullNameMaker 'struct' instance
    public employeeBenefit ()    // constructor method - same name as class
    {
        initializeComponents ();
        getEmployeeFullName ();    // call the method that gets employee full name
    }
    // this method uses the structure 'fullNameMaker' to create a list of employees full names
    private void getEmployeeFullName ()
    {
        employeeFullNameList.Clear ();   // initialize the list to spaces/null
        while (Reader.read)        // while the database still has employee records
        {
            fullName.firstName = databaseRecord.firstName;
            fullName.middleName = databaseRecord.middleName;
            fullName.lastName = databaseRecord.lastName;
            employeeFullName = fullName.organizeFullName ();
            employeeFullNameList.Add (employeeFullName);   // load the employees
        }
    }
} // end of employeeBenefit class
```

The above example assumes that the database records have fields/properties called firstName, middleName and lastName.

EXCEPTION USER-DEFINED DATA TYPE DECLARATION

Exception is an advanced user-defined data type feature in modern programming languages like C# that guarantees code execution during run time. This feature manages and controls all possible unexpected situations with meaningful messages to assist the end-user in case of application run interrupts, which prevent the application from continuing to run. C# uses the **'try'**, **'catch'**, and **'finally'** keywords to accomplish this feature. The following shows the exception syntax (format):

```
try
{
//   check for something
}
catch
{
//   display specific error message
}
finally
{
//   display general error message to avoid system crush
}
```

The following example demonstrates how you use the *'Exception'* user-defined data type in application:

```
using System.Windows.Forms;      // need it for MessageBox.Show method
using System.Data.SqlClient;     // Reader.read method is this namespace
public class sampleExceptionUsage
{
    string userName =   "JamesOkloo@gmail.com";
    public sampleExceptionUsage ()      // constructor – same name as class
    {
        checkDatabaseRecords ();   // call a method that checks for database records
    }
    private void checkDatabaseRecords ()
    {
        try
        {
                if (Reader.read)     // that is if we get first record, we are fine
                {
                    MessageBox.Show ("There are records in the database");
                    return;
                }
                MessageBox.Show ("There are no records in the database");
                return;
        }
        catch (System.Exception ex)
        {
                MessageBox.Show ("No database connection " + ex.ToString());
        }
        finally
        {
                // display general error that avoids system crush
```

```
            MessageBox.Show ("Contact the Database Administrator");
        }
    } /* end of loadRecords method */
} // end of sampleExceptionUsage class
```

ENUMERATIONS USER-DEFINED DATA TYPE DECLARATION

Enumeration is another important user-defined data type feature in object-oriented programming languages. It provides the functionality for the programmer to create enumerated values with a specific data type. In C# you can declare an enumeration data type using the *'enum'* compiler keyword and you access members using the dot notation (**.**). The following shows enumeration format declaration:

```
enum enumeratiionIdentifier
{
    enumerated list
}
```

The following example demonstrates how you use the 'Enumeration' user-defined data type in application: As every data type, you create a variable of that type in order to use the operations of the data type:

```
using System.Windows.Forms;      // need it for MessageBox.Show method
public class sampleEnumerationUsage
{
    enum WeekDays
    {
        Monday, Tuesday, Wednesday, Thursday,   Friday, Saturday, Sunday
    }
    public sampleEnumerationUsage ()    // constructor – same name as class
    {
        displayDayName ();   // call a method to display name of a day
    }
    private void displayDayName ()
    {
        WeekDays today;  // today is declared variable of WeekDays enum
        string todayName = today.Saturday;
    }
} // end of sampleEnumerationUsage class
```

C# KEYWORDS

As explained in Chapter 2, keywords are predefined reserved identifiers (names) that have special meanings to the compiler. They can't be used as identifiers (variable names) in your program. The following table contains most of the C# keywords:

abstract	as	base	bool	break	byte
case	catch	delegate	unchecked	protected	stackalloc
namespace	decimal	interface	default	readonly	foreach
public	checked	if	params	using	continue
true	ushort	int	internal	sbyte	sizeof
private	false	new	switch	unsafe	volatile
finally	object	throw	sealed	override	struct
ulong	while	implicit	operator	extern	long
explicit	short	out	string	uint	virtual
ref	float	enum	event	typeof	is
lock	this	goto	class	return	try
const	else	fixed	for	double	do
char	double	static	null	in	

For example, the following statements will confuse the C# compiler and will be flagged as a warning/error:

```
int struct = 0;         // I'm declaring an integer variable to use in my program
string override = "Hey, buddy — watch out. I think the C# Compiler is watching you! ";
```

In the above statements, both '**struct**' and '**override**' are predefined reserved keywords that have a special meaning to the compiler, so don't use them to declare the variable in your program. On the other hand, you can declare your variables as follows without having any issue with the compiler.

```
int myStruct = 0;     // I'm declaring an integer variable to use in my program
string myOverride = "Always initialize your variables before you use them";
```

C# OPERATOR IDENTIFIERS (SYMBOLS)

The following table shows some of the basic operators used in arithmetical and logical operations for data processing in the central processing unit (CPU):

Operator	Purpose	Example

+	For arithmetic addition. This can be used by other data types, especially the string data type. It's termed as the overloaded operator.	`int total = (numOne + numTwo);`
		`char abc = ('A' + 'B' + 'C');`
		`string fullName = ("firstName" + " " + "lastName");`

-	For arithmetic subtraction	`decimal currBal = (actBal - withdrawnAmount);`
*	For arithmetic multiplication	`int result = (numOne * numTwo);`
/	For arithmetic division	`int result = (bigNumber / smallNumber);`
=	To assign a value to a variable	`int studentAge = 21;   float studentGPA = 3.0;` `string studentName = "Abiiba Atoh";`
==	For logical equation (i.e. equal to)	`if (studentGPA == 4.0)` `    MessageBox.Show ("Hi, you have schorlaship");`
>	Greater than during logical comparison	`if (accountBalance > 500000)` `    MessageBox.Show ("Your loan is approved");`
>=	Greater than or equal to for logical comparison	`if (studentGPA >= 3.8)` `    MessageBox.Show ("Congratulations Student");`
<	Less than during comparison	`if (studentGPA < 4.0)` `    MessageBox.Show ("You may apply next year");`
<=	Less than or equal to for logical comparison	`if (studentGPA <= 3.0)` `    MessageBox.Show ("Contact admission office");`
!=	Not equal to during logical comparison	`if (userResponse (!= "yes")` `    Console.WriteLine ("Key in 'yes' - try again!");`
& and &&	'And'. Used for logical relations	`if ((studentAGE == 21) & (studentGPA == 4.0))` `    MessageBox.Show ("Contact housing office");`
| and ||	'Or'. Used for logical relations	`if ((studentGPA == 3.5) || (studentGPA > 3.5))` `    MessageBox.Show ("Hello, you are admitted");`

C# PROGRAM CONTROL FLOW

The following are some of the program control flows in C#:

ITERATION (LOOPING) STATEMENTS

The following section describes most of the C# iteration statements with examples:

'WHILE' LOOP STATEMENT

The 'while' loop is used to repeat the same expression until a specific condition is satisfied. The basic syntax (format) is as follows:

```
while (condition still not satisfied)
      continue to loop
```

The following example demonstrates how to use the 'while' loop statement in application:

```
using System;
namespace myConsoleApp
{
    class Program
    {
        static void Main(string[ ] args)
        {
            string response = " ";
            while (response != "Yes")
            {
                Console.WriteLine ("Key in 'Yes' – press Enter:");
                response = Console.ReadLine();
            }
            Console.WriteLine ("You keyed 'Yes' – Have a nice day.");
            Console.ReadLine ();
        }
    } // end of Program class
} // end of myConsoleApp namespace
```

'FOR' LOOP STATEMENT

The 'for' loop statement is used to perform a specific task continuously until a predefined limit is reached. The basic syntax (format) is as follows:

```
for (initial integer data type value counter; test decision limit; increase counter by 1)
    perform a specific task
```

The following example shows how to use the 'for' loop statement in application:

```
using System;
namespace myConsoleApp
{
    class Program
    {
      static void Main(string[ ] args)
      {
          string [ ] topStudents = { "George Coban", "James  Ankobea", "Marcus Modlinski" };
          Console.WriteLine ( "These top students have been awarded full scholarship!\n" );
          for (int countStudent = 0; countStudent <  topStudents.Length; ++countStudent)
          {
              Console.WriteLine (topStudents[countStudent]);  // print list of students
          }
          Console.WriteLine (" ");
          Console.ReadLine ();
      }
    }
}
```

The following result will appear after the application is run:

```
These top students have been awarded full scholarship!
George Coban
James Ankobea
Marcus Modlinski
```

'FOREACH' LOOP STATEMENT

The 'foreach' loop statement is an enhancement of the 'for' loop statement. It simplifies the 'for' loop statement syntax dramatically. It's generally used to iterate on all of the items in a   collection. The syntax (format) is as follows:

```
foreach (datatype in the collection of same datatype)
        do something
```

The following console application shows how to use the 'foreach' loop statement:

```
using System;
namespace myConsoleApp
{
    class Program
    {
      static void Main(string[ ] args)
      {
```

```
        string[ ] topStudents = { "George Coban", "James   Ankobea", "Marcus Modlinski" };
        Console.WriteLine ("These top students have been awarded full scholarship.\n");
        foreach (string student in topStudents)
        {
            Console.WriteLine (student);  // display the student name on the command line
        }
        Console.WriteLine (" ");
        Console.ReadLine ();
    }
  }
}
```

This will be the result when the application is run:

```
These top students have been awarded full scholarship!
George Coban
James Ankobea
Marcus Modlinski
```

CONDITIONAL STATEMENTS

The following section describes some of the C# conditional statements with examples:

'IF' CONDITIONAL STATEMENT

The 'if' statement is used in logical conditional statements to test conditions for true or false so that decisions can be made to achieve results during data processing. The syntax (format) is   as follows:

```
if   (this situation is true)
        then perform this specific task
else
        don't perform this task
```

The following static *testClass* class uses the *testIfStatement* method to show how to use the 'if' conditional statement in application:

```
using System.Windows.Forms;   // MessageBox.Show () is in the 'Forms' class
namespace MyWindowsApp
{
    public static class testClass
    {
      public static void testIfStatement (float studendGPA)    // call me with your GPA
      {
```

```
        MessageBox.Show ("Hi Reader, I'm the 'if' statement testing method.");
        if (studendGPA > 3.8)
        {
            MessageBox.Show ("Congratulation, you have been admitted...");
        }
        else
            MessageBox.Show ("Hello, contact the admissions office...");
    }
  }
}
```

The following shows how to use the *'testIfStatement'* method in your application for all student grade point averages to determine their admission to a specific college.

```
using System.Data.SqlClient;      // Reader.read method is this namespace
public class abcCollegeGPAadmissionCriteria
{
    private float studentGPA = 0.0f;      // variable to store individual student's GPA
    public abcCollegeGPAadmissionCriteria ()    // the constructor for this class
    {
        studentsApplication ();   // calling studentsApplication method
    }
    private void studentsApplication ()
    {
        while (Reader.read)
        {
            studentGPA = databaseRecord.StudentGPA;
            testClass.testIfStatement (studentGPA);      // calling testIfStatement method
        }
    }
} // end of abcCollegeGPAadmissionCriteria class
```

'SWITCH' CONDITIONAL STATEMENT

The 'switch' statement is used to create a very simple conditional statement syntax to reduce the complexities of several levels of the 'if' statements in a program during logical analysis for decision-making purposes. The syntax (format) is as follows:

```
switch (variable-name)
    case 'current content in variable-name': //  'case' is a keyword for testing conditions
        perform some specific task
        break;    // 'break' is the keyword used to exit the switch conditional testing
    default:  // 'default' is used when variable-name is not one of the 'case'
        say or do something
        break;
```

The following 'static testClass' class uses the *testSwitchStatement* method to show how to use the 'switch' conditional statement in application:

```
using System.Windows.Forms;   // needed for MessageBox.Show method
namespace MyWindowsApp
{
    public static class testClass
    {
     public static void testSwitchStatement(string countryName)    // call me with a country
      {
        MessageBox.Show ("Hi, call me from any class to test the 'switch' statement.");
        switch (countryName)        // the  switch statement in use
        {
           case "Canada":
           MessageBox.Show ("Capital of  " + countryName +  " is Ottawa in Ontario");
           break;
           case "United   States of America":
           MessageBox.Show ("Capital of " + countryName +  " is   Washington DC");
           break;
           case "United   Kingdom":
           MessageBox.Show ("Capital of  " + countryName +  " is London in England");
           break;
           default:
           MessageBox.Show ("Hi, I don't know the capital of  " +   countryName);
           break;
        }
      }
    }
}
```

The following is how you use the *testSwitchStatement* method in your application for listing capital cities in all the countries in the world:

```
using System.Data.SqlClient;      // Reader.read method is in this namespace
public class countriesCapital
{
    private string countryName = " ";    // string variable to store country names
    public countriesCapital ()    // the constructor for this class
    {
        countriesDatabase ();   // calling countriesDatabase method
    }
    private void countriesDatabase ()
    {
        while (Reader.read)
```

```
        {
            countryName = databaseRecord.Country;
            testClass.testSwitchStatement (countryName);
        }
    }
} // end of countriesCapital class
```

TRANSFER CONTROL STATEMENTS

Transfer control statements are used to transfer situations in a logical analysis condition in a program to a predefined location somewhere in a program. Good programming practice always discourages using transfer statements since it creates ambiguity in the program flow (especially in a large project where different programmers are working on the same program). The following section shows some of C# control transfer statements:

'RETURN' TRANSFER STATEMENT

The 'return' statement returns a result from a method that performs a specific task in a program. The following 'static testClass' class example uses the *testReturnStatement*'method to show how to use the 'return' control statement in application. The *testReturnStatement*' method creates a full name and returns the result to any caller in a project that calls this method with first name and last name as parameters:

```
using System;
namespace MyWindowsApp
{
    public static class testClass
    {
      private string fullName = " ";
      public static string testReturnStatement (string firstName, string lastName)
      {
          fullName = (firstName + " " +  lastName);
          return fullName;   // leave this method and give full name to the caller
      }
    }
}
```

The following is how you use the above testReturnStatement method anywhere in your application:

```
using System;
public class namesOrganizer
```

```
{
    private string firstName = "Alicia ", lastName = "Adams ", fullName =   " ";
    public namesOrganizer ()       // I'm the constructor for this class
    {
        fullName = testClass.testReturnStatement (firstName, lastName);
        MessageBox.Show ("Hi, your full name   is " + fullName);
    }
} // end of namesOrganizer class
```

The 'fullName' variable content after the call to *testReturnStatement* method in 'testClass' class after the 'MessageBox.Show () method will be as follows:

Hi, your full name is Alicia Adams

'BREAK' TRANSFER STATEMENT

The 'break' statement is used to search for specific criteria in a list of data items and if the data item is found, then the search is stopped. The following example is a method in an application that reads the current year's college admission database to look for at least one foreign student:

```
using System.Windows.Forms;     // MessageBox.Show() is in this namespace
using System.Data.SqlClient;     // Reader.read is in this namespace
namespace MyWindowsApp
{
    public static class testClass
    {
        private string studentAdmissionStatus   = " ", studentName = " ";
        public static string testBreakStatement ()
        {
            while (Reader.read)
            {
                studentAdmissionStatus =   databaseRecord.studentStatus;
                studentName = databaseRecord.studentName;
                If   (studentAdmissionStatus == "foreign")
                {
                    break;     // stop reading the admissions database – out of the loop
                    return   studentName;   // leave this method
                }
            }
            return "no";   // no foreign student this year
        }
    }
}
```

The following is how you use the 'testBreakStatement' method in any class in your project:

```
public class studentsAnnualAdmissionsMonitor   // a class in a University System App
{
    private string studentName = " ";
    public studentsAnnualAdmissionsMonitor ()   // I'm the constructor for this class
    {
      studentName = testClass.testBreakStatement ();   // no parameters passed
      if (studentName != "no")
      {
          MessageBox.Show ("Welcome  " + studentName + "  to our College!");
      }
      else
          MessageBox.Show ("Unfortunately, no foreign students this year");
    }
}
```

UNDERSTANDING VISUAL STUDIO SOFTWARE DEVELOPMENT KIT

As explained earlier in this chapter, the Microsoft Visual Studio Software Development Kit/Tool is a system software that collaborates with the Microsoft .NET Framework to make application system development extremely easy. The Visual Studio Software architecture provides a development environment that creates a well-defined structure for application development. A typical application is contained in a 'solution', this solution is a container for one or more projects. A project contains one or more classes (usually your project's name will be the same as the name of your solution and 'namespace', but you can always change the solution or the project name). C# applications are normally developed using .NET Framework and the Visual Studio Software Development tool. To create a new C# application, you need to have the Visual Studio Development Kit installed on your computer system. Refer to the 'System Requirements' in this book for the necessary installation links. Launch whatever version you have on your computer and you will see the 'Start Page'. If you have Microsoft Visual C# 2010 Express installed on your computer, the following 'Start Page' (figure 1) will appear when you launch it.

Select the 'New Project' option and the following environment (figure 2) will appear.

Select the C# and 'Windows Forms Application' options from the Installed Templates. Enter the name of your project, for instance 'MyWindowsApp' (this will be the default name

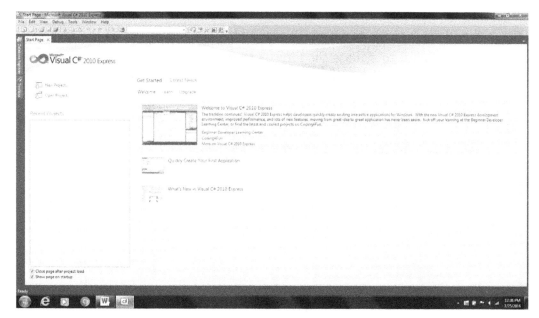

Figure 1. Visual Studio Start Page

Figure 2. Visual Studio New Project Template

for your solution, project and namespace), then click 'OK'. The following environment (*Figure 3*) will appear with its default Windows form design size and all the properties and events (methods) to manage the form as shown in figure 3. This Windows design form is the user-interface for your application system audience.

Figure 3. Visual Studio Windows Application Form Design Environment

You can change the default Windows size to suit your needs by playing with the properties of the Windows form at the bottom right of the window (the events and properties window). Now find the 'Tool Box' item on the menu bar and click on it. Then find 'Solution' on the items menu bar and click on it. Enlarge the design form, and the following typical Windows application form design environment provided by Visual Studio and the .NET Framework will appear as shown in figure 4.

The window on the left is the 'Tool Box' window that has all the classes you need to create instances in your Windows application. You can drag and drop any object like, 'button', 'comboBox', or 'images' onto your 'form' and design them to suit your audience. The above design form has 'label', 'textbox', 'radiobutton', 'checkbutton' and two

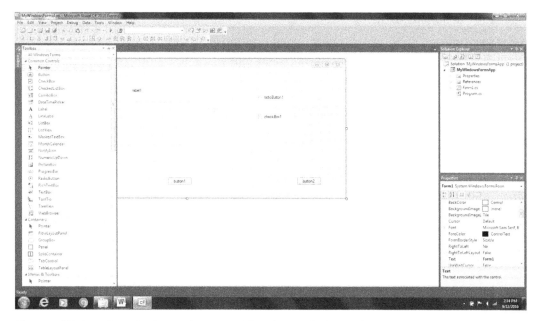

Figure 4. Windows Forms Design Environment with ToolBox, Solution, and Properties Windows

'button' objects. The top right window lists your 'Solution' and the 'Project(s)' in that solution, and the Project(s) list all the files in each project. You can work on any of these files by selecting it (double clicking on it). The bottom right window provides all the properties and events for a particular object at that time. For instance, if you drag and drop a 'button' object onto the design form, Visual Studio in collaboration with the .NET Framework will automatically generate all the applicable events and properties for the 'button' object.

Now close the 'Tool Box', and double click on the design form, the following environment will appear as shown in figure 5. This is the environment that the Visual Studio in collaboration with the .NET Framework Class Library automatically generates code that provides the basic 'namespaces' with classes that the application type will need support services based on the selected project template. There are different .NET Framework Class Library support services for 'Console Project', 'Windows Project', 'Internet Project', etc. This environment is a Windows Forms project, and here, you can implement the behavior of all events, add all fields, properties and methods to provide all the logic for this class as part of the application. One extremely useful feature provided by the Visual

Studio is the built-in artificial intelligence functionalities in the text editor. The editor helps you to learn of all of the public members of any data type, just type the name of the data type and press the dot (.) character and the editor will automatically list all the members in that type for you.

Figure 5. Text Editor for Coding in Visual Studio Development Environment

When you're in this environment, you can add any number of Windows forms, classes and every object you need by opening the 'Project' menu bar and choosing the item you want to add to your project. For instance, to add another Windows design form to your project, select the *'Add Windows Form'* option. To add a new class to this project, we'll select the *'Add Class'* option on the 'Project' menu bar and the following environment will appear as shown in figure 6.

You can give any name to your new class. When you click the 'Add' button, the following screen will appear as shown in figure 7. You can then decorate your class to suit the purpose of the class, whether you want to use it as a 'sealed', 'static', or 'abstract' class. This is the environment you'll provide to all of the members and their behavior and access privileges to all of the clients in your application.

Figure 6. Add new item to project template Environment.

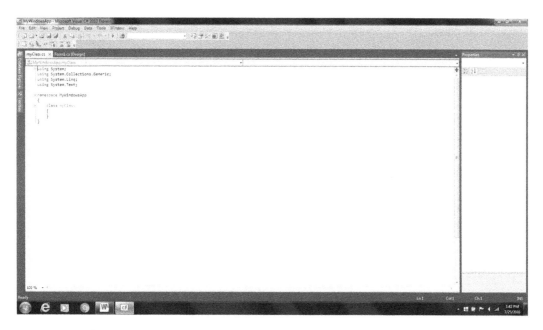

Figure 7. New Class Editing Environment

COMPILING AND RUNNING YOUR APPLICATION

After you've finished designing your user-interface windows forms and have completed all the codes in your classes, you have to compile and run your application to make sure that it's doing what you intend it to do. Visual Studio makes it easy to compile and run your programs. Just click on 'Debug' on the menu bar and select *'StartDebugging'*. If you get syntax errors, they'll all be listed in another window for you to let you correct them, so that you can compile your programs again.

WHAT HAVE YOU LEARNED?

- Microsoft's .NET Framework allows you to quickly and easily code a program using any supported language.

- C# makes use of user-defined data types, but in the .NET Framework you're able to reference a library of predefined functions making coding even easier.

- When defining a class, you're deciding who or what will be able to access and use that class.

- Managing methods in C# is what allows you to define what functions do and how they behave.

- Different types of statements can be used to create more complex functions that will be activated when predefined criteria are met.

- The Microsoft Visual Studio Software Development Kit works in conjunction with .NET Framework to further simplify coding and give you a visual interface to use.

PART II

INTRODUCING APPLICATION SYSTEM DEVELOPMENT

This part introduces the application system development process. It explains the various parts that should be available before a software product can be developed. It explains all the necessary processes needed before an application system can be functional. It describes systems analysis and design, hardware platforms, operating systems, programming languages, coding (i.e., program writing), testing, implementation/deployment, software development environment tools etc., that support the overall goal of application system development.

CHAPTER 4

WHAT IS THE BASIC SOFTWARE DEVELOPMENT PROCESS?

The very first step in developing any piece of software is deciding what its purpose is. What is it that you want the computer to do for you? Generally, software can do anything that a human would do on a computer, but more quickly and efficiently. So, what is your goal for your software?

One goal could be managing your monthly bills. With this goal in mind, you might create a financial application that links with your bank account and the different companies you pay each month, and the software will automatically make your monthly payments.

Next, you need to decide what kind of people will use your applications. Who are they? What problem are you solving for them? What's their level of technical expertise? Understanding this will help you to make good decisions when it's time to develop your software.

For our example of a bill payment application, the end user might be the head of a household, or perhaps an older person who doesn't want to forget to pay their bills, so they decide to automate them. Once you have an idea of this, you can make specific decisions about how our software will look and what it will do.

The next step, is analyzing the application system and imagining how it could be designed. Think about your final goals for the system. Then create development guidelines to make sure you reach those goals.

After this, you need to choose your target hardware or development platform. This depends on what your users are most likely to set up bill pay on. Is it a PC, Mac, or mobile device? Deciding this will help you to make other key decisions later on.

Finally, you need to choose a programming language. This decision will be based on a variety of factors. The main thing you need to be sure of is that the programming language is able to communicate in the proper machine code.

ANALYZING AND DESIGNING YOUR APPLICATION SYSTEM

The decisions that you've already made give you the criteria that your application must meet, but they have little to do with its actual design. So now, you need to take the time to analyze the system and design how it will work and be used.

One simple way to do this is creating a flowchart for how your application will behave. The flowchart will show the logical flow of the user's interactions with the application. This can help you identify any potential challenges in advance, so that you can devise solutions, and it will also serve as your outline during the coding phase.

It's also important to determine the data types and data sources that you'll be working with. Will it be a file, database, Internet-based, or command line system? Will it work with mathematical and scientific formulas or will it merely organized data? Asking these questions will give you a better understanding of what capabilities your programming language and development environment will need.

Also, take time to consider the input and output of your application. By input, we mean the data that the application will receive to perform a process on and provide the output. So, your input data might come from a database or may be entered by the user themselves. This will all depend on the specific application that you're developing. The output will be the result of the process. Generally, the whole purpose of an application will be to receive the output.

CHOOSING A DEVELOPMENT PLATFORM

When choosing a development platform, the first question you need to ask is: who is your end-client? If it's a government organization, then your software may be housed on a large mainframe computer. If it's a small company that uses networked servers, then your application needs to be lighter. Next decide which hardware platform and operating system will be best for your application. At times, a hardware platform will have multiple operating systems installed, so it's important to determine this before you start developing.

When thinking of potential operating systems, try to find one that meets the following criteria:

- The operating system must be able to communicate with the hardware platform.

- The operating system must be able to understand your intended programming language without unnecessary intermediaries.

- The operating system either comes preinstalled on the hardware platform or can be easily installed on it.

Based on this criteria, you can create a pro-con list for each development platform, to choose the best option.

CHOOSING A PROGRAMMING LANGUAGE

The next decision to make, is which programming language you'll use to create your application. This really depends on what you want the software to do. For example, if you're creating an engineering application, you might use FORTRAN since it has many complex mathematical formulas built in. This will save quite a bit of work for you as the programmer. On the other hand, if you wanted to make a simple version of the game Pong, then you could use C# or Java.

Another important decision is what development kit you'll use. The development kit is where you'll type and test your code, so you need to make sure it's up to this challenge. For example, if you were going to make a Pong game in C#, then you might use Visual Studio as your development environment since it's designed for use with C# and provides all of the needed functionalities. As you code the application, you'll be able to test, and even run, your application.

Different programming languages work better with certain development kits, so make sure to choose one that will be adequate for your needs.

GETTING TO WORK

Now that you've carefully researched and chosen the best approach for your application, it's time to start coding it. This process may take just a few months for a small application, to a few years for a larger application. At times fifteen or more programmers may be working on an application simultaneously to get it done in time. This is where the majority of your time will be spent on any application.

After the application is coded, you'll need to compile it. If you remember, the compiler is the guy who translates alphanumeric characters into binary code. This lets the computer understand the code that you've written.

The compiler will also make sure that your code follows the laws of the language. So, if there are syntax errors, these will stop the compiler before it can finish its work. When the compiler stops, you'll have a clue as to where the syntax errors are, so you can fix them and try to compile the code again.

Now, even if your program compiles correctly, it doesn't mean that it will show the results that you want. So, if your program is showing the incorrect result, what does that mean? That means there's a semantics error in the code. The semantics are the logical part of the code that allows the application to serve its purpose. For example, an accounting programming might add together accounts instead of subtracting them like you intended, this would be a logic problem. So, if there are any logical errors in the application after it has been compiled, then take the time to debug these.

Finally, after your rounds of testing and debugging, it's time to run the application. At this point, your application still shouldn't be considered final, since there's still more work to do before it's ready.

The last step in your software development process is user testing. During this phase, you'll want have a potential end-user test the software to see if it serves its purpose well. Is the user able to easily access the functions they need? Does the program design and logic make sense? How does it compare with their current software solution? These are all excellent questions that user testing can answer. With these answers in hand, you'll be able to fine-tune your application and finalize it.

WHAT HAVE YOU LEARNED?

- Researching things about your target hardware platform, programming language, and software development kit, will save time during the coding phase.

- The majority of your time will be spent on the initial coding phase.

- After coding, there's a compilation phase where you correct syntax errors (following a programming language's rules) and a debugging phase to fix semantic (logical) errors.

- User testing is a very useful step that helps you to ensure that the application meets user needs.

PART III

INTRODUCING PROGRAM AND DATA ACCESS

This part introduces computer program and data access. Every application system uses some type of data. How data is accessed and saved by a program is thoroughly explained. Two of the most common data access methods (the File System and the Relational Database Management System) are explained with extensive practical examples.

CHAPTER 5

WHAT IS DATA ACCESS?

Computer programming is meaningless if there's no data to work with. Almost all real-life computer application systems use some form of data. This is actually the main reason why computers were invented, to manage data so that the user has accurate information available to them in order to make decisions. Therefore, data plays a key role in application system development because most applications that are developed access data and/or save data.

In this chapter, we'll discuss how computer programs use the *"File System"* data access methodology to save data (write data to storage devices) and access data (read or retrieve data from storage devices), for use by the CPU during conditional and logical processing. This allows the computer to achieve the user's desired result. As the programmer, you must therefore fully understand the concept of data access using the *"File System"*.

Most high-level programming languages, such as COBOL, FORTRAN, Pascal, C, C++, CLU, Java, and C#, come with built-in features that use meaningful verbs to achieve this objective without the programmer needing to learning how to use low-level languages (assembly or machine language) to manipulate data directly on a physical storage device (tapes or disks). As a computer programmer, you should look for these features in any language that you're interested in using to develop your software. The following table contains most of the identifiers (features) that high-level programming languages use to manipulate data during programming using the *'File System'*. These verbs are functions with parameters used to define and manipulate data in the *'File System'* data access methodology.

Statement Name	Purpose
create	The 'create' statement is used to create a new library/directory/folder or a new file.
open	The 'open' statement receives a parameter with a file identifier (name) and uses it to establish a connection to the file's location on the storage device (usually on a disk/tape). The file must exist, otherwise the 'open' statement will return an error message.
read	The 'read' statement is used to retrieve records from a file with or without certain conditions. This function can only be used if and only if the 'open' function is activated.
seek	The 'seek' statement is used to locate a record based on conditions by using a unique field in a file record. This function can only be used if and only if the 'open function is activated.
write	The 'write' statement is used to add a new record to an existing file. This function can only be used if and only if the file is in an open mode.
rewrite/update	The 'rewrite' or 'update' statement is used normally after the read or seek statements to make changes to specific field(s) in a record(s). This function can only be used if the file exists and is already opened.
delete	The 'delete' statement is used to remove a record or group of records from a file. The file must already exist and already be open. This statement is also used to delete existing library/directory/folders or existing files.
close	The 'close' statement is used to disconnect the link that the open statement established with the file. The file must exist and already be open.

Most programming languages will use these verbs to manipulate data; however, there are no standardized statements for handling data, because each language uses its own variations. To learn how to manipulate data in a programming language, you need to learn how it uses these verbs to make statements.

There's also systems software that's been developed to make the programmer's life easier by creating a very high-level language data access protocol between programs and data access to make the data definition and manipulation extremely simple (an improvement on the *'File System'*). This way, data can be accessed using features built by the programming languages creators. This systems software is developed by systems programmers, and they come with their own unique language syntax that allows high-level programming languages to manipulate data in a very simple way. For instance, they come with built-in sorting, searching, and projection functionalities that take the burden off of the programmer by creating these algorithms. To use the language, the computer programmer has to understand how to use the syntax of the language in order to embed these into a computer program. These data access protocol systems that offer easy data definitions and manipulations are usually called *'Database Management Systems'*.

Most programming language designers and compiler creators make provisions to accommodate these foreign data sub-languages from the Database Management Systems. At the time of writing this book, the most common among these data manipulation support systems software are Network Database Management System, Hierarchical Database Management System, Relational Database Management System and Object-Oriented Database Management System. Currently, as an applications programmer, most of the software you build will be done using the most popular Relational Database Management System as your data access tool. chapter 6 discusses Database Management Systems using the Relational Database Management System as a case study.

THE FILE SYSTEM

For a computer program to have access to data, the programmer must know the name and location of the data on a specific storage device. The *'File System'* is a member of a group of file 'Input' and 'Output' methodologies in computer science known as *'Stream'* (an abstraction of a process where data is stored on a device in a linear fashion and accessed/retrieved the same way, one byte at a time. The device can be a memory location, a network channel, a disk file or any other device that uses a linear approach for reading and writing to it). The *'File System'* uses the *'disk file stream'* approach.

In computer programming the *'File System'* is how files are organized on a storage device so that they can be accessed by computer programs. This is based on computer science (specifically data structures) concept of a tree or hierarchical data structure where all of the branches of a tree come from one root, and branches can have their own branches and continue growing with more branches until it gets to the leaves (which is usually called the nodes) and more trees are therefore known as the forest (i.e., several tree roots clustered in the same place with unique identifiers). This is the concept used to create several root libraries/directories/folders on the same storage device, but with each root library/directory/folder having a unique identifier (name).

In big computers, like mainframes and mini computers that are used to store large amounts of data, the file system uses the term 'libraries' with unique identifiers to store data and provide information on the location of each library on a storage device (usually on tapes or disks). Using the tree hierarchical structure concept, a root library or a parent library can have several sub-libraries and a sub-library can have several sub-sub-libraries and files, etc. There can be several root libraries on the same storage device, but each should have a unique root name. These unique libraries contain the sub-libraries that contain the files that the computer program works with.

In most personal computer systems with operating systems, like DOS (Disk Operating System), Windows, Macintosh and Unix/Linux-based operating systems, the file system is usually called directories or folders. The directory/folder is a container and the members in the container are sub-directories/folders and files with unique identifiers (names). In the directory/sub-directory file system, every sub-directory/folder usually contains folders and files. Some of the common files in the sub-directory/folder are programs, data, text, images, audio, or video, each belonging to a unique folder. For instance, an image folder will only contain image files, a text folder will only contain text files, a data folder will only contain data files, etc.

THE 'PATH' SYSTEM

Most of the file system structures in Windows and Unix/Linux-based operating systems use the 'Path' system to locate a sub-directory/folder or files on the storage device starting from the root directory. The 'Path' system uses the back slash character ' \ ' to separate a sub-directory from its root/parent directory and a file from its root/parent directory/sub-directory. For this system to function efficiently, the 'Path' system enforces unique identifiers (names) for all members under one directory/sub-directory/folder container. Thus, you can't have two sub-directories with the same name in a parent directory container, and you can't have two files with the same name in the same directory/sub-directory/folder container. On the other hand, you can have the same name for different sub-directories/files in different directories/sub-directories containers and you can have the same file names in different directory/sub-directory containers. The following example demonstrates the *'Path'* system structure. For instance to locate the file *'image1.jpeg'* in the sub-directory *'ImagesDirectory'* of *'RootDirectoryOne'*, you have to traverse through the *'Path'* from *'RootDirectoryOne'* through *'ImagesDirectory'* by separating each with the backslash character ' \ ' until you reach the file *'image1.jpeg'* (i.e., the node/leaf of the tree).

```
Example-1:     C:\RootDirectoryOne\ImagesDirectory\image1.jpeg
Example-2:     C:\RootDirectoryTwo\ImagesDirectory\image1.jpeg
Example-3:     C:\RootDirectoryOne\ImagesDirectory\image1.jpeg
```

In the above examples, the *'RootDirectoryOne'* directory/folder in *'Example-3'* has a duplicate name, because there's a root library/directory/folder with the same name that already exists on the same storage device (i.e., the C drive). The only way you can create a root directory with the same name is to delete the existing one. *'RootDirectoryOne'* can't have any sub-directory/folder with the same name as *'ImagesDirectory'*, but note that the same name *'ImagesDirectory'* is allowed to be in *'RootDirectoryTwo'*. Also, note that the image file *'image1.jpeg'* is used in both *'RootDirectoryOne'* sub-directory *'ImagesDirectory'* and *'RootDirectoryTwo'* sub-directory *'ImagesDirectory'* with no problem. But, you can't have another *'image1.jpeg'* file in any of the *'ImagesDirectory'* sub-directory of their respective root directories. The *'File System'* doesn't allow duplicate names in the same library/directory/folder/sub-directory container on the same storage device.

C#.NET AND DATA ACCESS

As mentioned in chapter 3, you are using the C# programming language to teach you how to write a computer program. C# is a very flexible and growing programming language. This is because C# is a completely Object-Oriented Programming Language and can easily adapt to any real-life application situation. At the time of writing this book, there are few C# data access protocols. This include the *'File System'*, XML (Extensible Markup Language), ADO.NET, LINQ (Language Integrated Query) and the Entity Framework. This book discusses the most basic and common C# data access, the *'File System'* and the ADO. NET with practical and applicable examples using the services of the .NET Framework Class Library.

C#.NET AND THE FILE SYSTEM

As explained in chapter 3, all C# applications target the .NET Framework because the .NET Framework assists, supports, and manages the C# source code and provides a run-time environment for program execution and deployment (in collaboration with the Visual Studio application system). The .NET Framework Class Library has a namespace called **'System.IO'** with classes that have all the functionalities to let you manage the 'File System' in your program. You can learn more about the file system classes by referring to the .NET Framework Class Library documentation on your computer or by visiting the Microsoft website and searching for the .NET Framework Class Library (specifically, the 'System.IO' namespace). Some of the common classes in the 'System.IO' namespace are the static *'Directory'* class - (with all the public properties and methods to manipulate and handle all directory/folder operations), the static *'File'* class (with all the public properties and methods to manipulate and handle all file operations), the *'StreamWriter'* class with functions to write record(s) to an existing file and *'StreamReader'* class with all the functions you need to read record(s) from an existing file. This section discusses some of the most common operations you'll be performing in your program through practical case studies. C# uses the *'Path'* system discussed earlier to manage directories/ sub-directories/folders and files.

HOW TO CREATE A DIRECTORY/SUB-DIRECTORY (FOLDER)

The following example demonstrates how a program dynamically creates a directory or sub-directory using the static **'CreateDirectory'** method in the static **'Directory'** class of the 'System.IO' namespace in the .NET Framework Class Library. In this example, the programmer has created a 'static' class called *'ManageFileSystem'* in an application to handle some common and basic standard file system operations to be used anywhere in an application. Remember that you don't create an instance of a static class; you only call it and use the dot notation (**.**) to access all public members of a static class; and also note that all members in a static class are decorated with the word 'static'.

```
using System.IO;     // Directory.CreateDirectory method is in this namespace
public static class ManageFileSystem
{
    private static string operationResult = " ";    // string variable to be used in this class only
    /* this method creates a new directory/subdirectory on the C drive. It accepts one parameter
    (i.e. 'the path' of the directory) and returns result to the caller */
    public static string createNewDirectory (string thePath)
    {
        try
        {
            Directory.CreateDirectory (thePath);      // using the 'CreateDirectory' method
            operationResult = "The directory " + thePath " successfully created ....";
        }
        catch (Exception ex)
        {
            operationResult = "Fatal error has occurred ..." + ex.ToString ();
        }
        return operationResult;
    }
        // place the rest of all the static methods members in this class here
} // end of ManageFileSystem class
```

You can use the above static *'createNewDirectory'* method to create any number of direc-
tories/sub-directories/folders in your application. The following example demonstrates
how you use the above static method *'createNewDirectory'* method in a class called *'App-
SystemOne'* in your windows application. C# uses the '@' character to precede a literal
string to tell the compiler that the following literal strings mean the same thing (i.e.,
@**"C:\asioTech"** is the same as **"C:\\asioTech"**).

```
using System;
using System.Windows.Forms;    // MessageBox.Show method is in this namespace
public class AppSystemOne
{
    private string thePath = " ", operationResult = " ";    // declaring string variables
    public AppSystemOne ()   // constructor  - call to create class  instance
    {
        InitializeComponents ();    // initialize all variables in this app
        createNewFolder ();         // call this private method to create folders
    }
    private void createNewFolder()
    {
        // create a root directory called 'asioTech' on the C drive
```

```
        thePath = @"C:\asioTech";
        operationResult = ManageFileSystem.createNewDirectory (thePath);
        MessageBox.Show (operationResult);
        // create a subdirectory called 'forData' in the 'asioTech' root directory
        thePath = @"C:\asioTech\forData";
        operationResult = ManageFileSystem.createNewDirectory (thePath);
        MessageBox.Show (operationResult);
        // create a subdirectory called 'forText' in the 'asioTech' root directory
        thePath = @"C:\asioTech\forText";
        operationResult = ManageFileSystem.createNewDirectory (thePath);
        MessageBox.Show (operationResult);
        // create a subdirectory called 'forImages' in the 'asioTech' root directory
        thePath = @"C:\asioTech\forImages";
        operationResult = ManageFileSystem.createNewDirectory (thePath);
        MessageBox.Show (operationResult);
    }
        // place the rest of AppSystemOne class members here ....
} // end of AppSystemOne class
```

As explained earlier on, an application system is one or several functions exchanging data and messages through parameters, so in the above private void the *'createNewFolder'* method, the statement:

```
operationResult = ManageFileSystem.createNewDirectory (thePath);
MessageBox.Show (operationResult);
```

calls the static *'createNewDirectory'* method in a static class known as *'ManageFileSystem'* with *'thePath'* parameter and returns the result of the method call into the string variable *'operationResult'* and uses the *'MessageBox.Show'* method in 'System.Windows.Forms' namespace to display the result in a Windows application.

HOW TO CREATE A FILE IN A DIRECTORY

The file is usually the node/leaf of the tree hierarchical structure. The file is the identifier on the *'Path'* system that actually contains the information like text, data, image, audio, and video that your application works with. The file therefore plays a very important role in the *'File System'*. A file must be created so that a computer program can use its content. There are different types of files: example program files (to contain program source codes), data files (to contain data), text files (to contain textual information), audio files (to contain audio), and video files (to contain video). The C# programming language has different methods to create and manipulate different types of files, and the .NET Framework Class Library makes them available to the programmer by using the **'System.IO'** namespace, which is available when you're developing your C# application through the Visual Studio Software Development tool. The following example shows how a program dynamically uses the static method *'CreateText'* in the static *'File'* class in the 'System.IO' namespace to create any text file in a specific directory/sub-directory to be used by all clients (classes) in an application:

```
using System;
using System.IO;        // File.CreateText method is in this namespace
public static class ManageFileSystem  // static class must not be instantiated
{
    private static string operationResult = " ";    // declaring private string variable
    /* this method creates a new text file. It accepts one parameter (i.e. the path) and
      returns result to the caller using the string variable 'operationResult' */
    public static string createTextFile (string thePath)
    {
        try
        {
            File.CreateText (thePath);    // using the 'file system' create function
            operationResult = "The file " + the Path  + " successfully created ... ";
        }
        catch (Exception ex)
        {
            operationResult = "Fatal error has occurred ... " + ex.ToString();
        }
            return operationResult;
    } // end of createTextFile method
} // end of ManageFileSystem class
```

The following *'AppSystemOne'* class uses the above static *'createTextFile'* method in the above static *'ManageFileSystem'* class to create a text file called *'txtMsgs.txt'* in the *'for-Text'* sub-directory of the *'asioTech'* root directory in an application:

```
using System;
using System.Windows.Forms;
public class AppSystemOne
{
    private string thePath = " ", operationResult = " ";  // declaring private string variables
    public AppSystemOne ()  // constructor  - call to create class instance
    {
```

```
        InitializeComponents ();    // initialize all project variables
        createNewTextFile ();        // call this private method to create the new file
    }
    private void createNewTextFile ()
    {
                thePath = @"C:\asioTech\forText\txtMsgs.txt";
                operationResult = ManageFileSystem.createTextFile (thePath);
                MessageBox.Show (operationResult);    // display a message after the operation
    }
} // end of AppSystemOne class
```

HOW TO OPEN A FILE

Before you can use data, you have to know the location and availability of the data. The .NET Framework Class Library's 'System.IO' namespace has the static class *'File'* with several public static methods that can be used to open different types of files. One of these static methods is *'OpenText'*. The following example shows how a program dynamically opens a text file. In this example, the private *'openExistingFile'* method in *'AppSystemOne'* class is being called by the *'AppSystemOne'* class constructor (method) to open an existing text file called *'txtMsgs.txt'* in the *'forText'* sub-directory/folder of the root directory *'asioTech'* on the C drive:

```
using System;
using System.IO;       // File.OpenText method is in this namespace
using System.Windows.Forms;
public class AppSystemOne
{
    private string thePath = @"C:\asioTech\forText\txtMsgs.txt";
    public AppSystemOne ()   // constructor  - call to create class instance
    {
        InitializeComponents ();    // initialize all project variables
        openExistingTextFile ();    // call this private method to open a file
    }
    private void openExistingFile ()
    {
        try
        {
            File.OpenText (thePath);
        }
        catch (Exception ex)
        {
            MessageBox.Show ("Fatal error has occurred.. " + ex.ToString ());
```

```
        }
    } // end of openExistingFile method
} // end of AppSystemOne class
```

HOW TO WRITE A RECORD TO A FILE

The 'System.IO' namespace has several classes used to write record(s) to different types of files. The following example uses the ***StreamWriter*** class's ***WriteLine*** method to demonstrate how a program dynamically writes record(s) one at a time from an array to a text file. In this example, the private 'writeNewRecord' method in 'AppSystemOne' class is being called by the 'AppSystemOne' class constructor (method) to write records to the 'txtMsgs.txt' file in the 'forText' sub-directory/folder of the root directory 'asioTech' on the C drive:

```
using System;
using System.IO;       // StreamWriter.WriteLine method is in this namespace
using System.Windows.Forms;
public class AppSystemOne
{
    private string thePath = @"C:\asioTech\forText\txtMsgs.txt";
    public AppSystemOne ()     // constructor  – call to create class instance
    {
        InitializeComponents ();    // initialize all project variables
        writeNewRecord ();              // call this method to write records to a file
    }
    private void writeNewRecord ()
    {
        string[ ] topStudents = { "Paapa Demitris", "Rowena Bright", "David Talata",
                                "Marcus Modlinski", "Abed Nana", "Fred Boateng" };
        try
        {
            using (StreamWriter stWriter = new StreamWriter (thePath))
            foreach (string student in topStudents)
            {
                stWriter.WriteLine (student);
            }
        }
        catch (Exception ex)
        {
            MessageBox.Show ("Fatal error has occurred ... " + ex.ToString());
        }
    } // end of writeNewRecord method

} // end of AppSystemOne class
```

HOW TO READ A RECORD FROM A FILE

Data is always kept on reliable storage devices, so that it can be retrieved at the right time. As a programmer, based on your data access privileges in your organization, you must know how to have access to any form of information either on a local computer, or a network system (where the data's on a server somewhere across the globe), so that your application will make that information available to the user. The 'System.IO' namespace has several classes used to read record(s) from different types of files. The following example uses the *'StreamReader'* class' *'ReadLine'* method to demonstrate how a program dynamically reads record(s) from a text file. In this example, the private *'readRecordsFromFile'* method in *'AppSystemOne'* class is being called by the *'AppSystemOne'* class constructor (method) to read records from the *'txtMsgs.txt'* in the *'forText'* sub-directory/folder of the root directory *'asioTech'* on the C drive.

```
using System;
using System.IO;   // StreamReader.ReadLine method is in this namespace
using System.Windows.Forms;
public class AppSystemOne
{
    private string thePath = @"C:\asioTech\forText\txtMsgs.txt";
    int totalStudents = 0;
    public AppSystemOne ()     // constructor  - call to create an instance of this class
    {
        InitializeComponents ();       // initialize all project variables
        readRecordsFromFile ();        // call this method to read records
    }
    private void readRecordsFromFile()
    {
        try
        {
            using (StreamReader stReader = new StreamReader (thePath))
            while ((studentName == stReader.ReadLine ()) != null)
            {
                totalStudents = (totalStudents + 1);
            }
            MessageBox.Show ("Total Students is. " + totalStudents);
        }
        catch (Exception ex)
        {
            MessageBox.Show ("Fatal error has occurred. " + ex.ToString());
        }
    } // end of readRecordsFromFile method
} // end of AppSystemOne class
```

HOW TO CLOSE A FILE

It's good programming practice to always close a file after you're done using it. Usually in local area networks and Internet programming environments, there are several clients accessing the same file simultaneously. You use the static *'Close'* method of the static *'File'* class in 'System.IO' to close a file. The following example shows how a program dynamically closes a file. In this example, the private *'closeExistingFile'* method in the 'AppSystemOne' class is being called by the 'AppSystemOne' class constructor (method) to close the 'txtMsgs.txt' file in the 'forText' sub-directory/folder of the root directory 'asioTech' on the C drive.

```
using System;
using System.IO;
using System.Windows.Forms;
public class AppSystemOne
{
    private string thePath = @"C:\asioTech\forText\txtMsgs.txt";
    public AppSystemOne ()     // constructor - call to create class instance
    {
        InitializeComponents ();          // initialize all project variables
        closeExistingFile ();        // call this method to close a file
    }
    private void closeExistingFile ()
    {
        try
        {
            var optf = File.OpenText (thePath);
            optf.Close ();
            MessageBox.Show ("txtMsgs.txt file successfully closed!");
        }
        catch (Exception ex)
        {
            MessageBox.Show ("Fatal Error has occurred  " + ex.ToString());
        }
    } // end of closeExistingFile method

} // end of AppSystemOne class
```

HOW TO DELETE A FILE FROM A DIRECTORY/FOLDER

Sometimes you'll want to delete a file from your application completely. You can use the static method *'Delete'* of the static class *'File'* in 'System.IO' namespace to accomplish this. The following example shows how a program dynamically deletes a file from a specific directory/folder:

```
using System;
using System.IO;         // File.Delete method is in this namespace
public static class ManageFileSystem  // static class – no constructor method
{
    private static string operationResult = " ";    // string variable to be used in this class
    /* this static method deletes existing file – it accepts one parameter (the path) and
       returns result to the caller  */
    public static string deleteFile (string thePath)
    {
        try
        {
            File.Delete (thePath);        // using the file system delete function
            operationResult = "The file " + thePath  + " successfully deleted ... ";
        }
        catch (Exception ex)
        {
            operationResult = "Fatal error has occurred ... " + ex.ToString();
        }
        return operationResult;
    } // end of deleteFile method
} // end of ManageFileSystem class
```

The following is how the ‘*AppSystemOne*’ class uses the static ‘***deleteFile***’ method in the above static ‘*ManageFileSystem*’ class to delete a text file called ‘*txtMsgs.txt*’ in the ‘*forText*’ sub-directory of the ‘*asioTech*’ root directory in an application:

```
using System;
using System.Windows.Forms;
public class AppSystemOne
{
    private string thePath = " ", operationResult = " ";     // declare string variables
    public AppSystemOne ()    // constructor  – call to create class instance
    {
        InitializeComponents ();       // initialize all project variables
        deleteExistingTextFile ();       // call this method to delete a file
    }
    private void deleteExistingTextFile ()
    {
        thePath = @"C:\asioTech\forText\txtMsgs.txt";
        /* call the ManageFileSystem's deleteFile method to delete 'thePath' file */
```

```
        operationResult = ManageFileSystem.deleteFile (thePath);
        MessageBox.Show (operationResult);
    }
} // end of AppSystemOne class
```

HOW TO DELETE A DIRECTORY/SUB-DIRECTORY (FOLDER)

Sometimes you'll want to delete a directory/folder or sub-directory from your application. For instance, if you've developed a new software product to sell, but you want potential customers to use your application free for 30 days. Your application will create a root directory, sub-directories and all the necessary files on the potential customers' computers to enable them to use the free, 30-day trial. Your application will normally give them the option to purchase your product or to decline after the trial period. Your application will automatically delete the root directory, all sub-directories and all files from the computers of all those potential customers who decline after the free, 30-day trial. The following example shows how a program dynamically deletes a root directory or sub-directory from the C drive using the static method '***Delete***' of the static class '***Directory***' in the 'System.IO' namespace. Normally, you'll want to check whether the directory/sub-directory exists or not by using the static 'Directory.Exists' method in the static 'Directory' class in the 'System.IO' namespace before you delete the directory.

```
using System.IO;      // Directory.Delete method is in this namespace
public static class ManageFileSystem
{
    private static string operationResult = " ";    // string variable to be used in this class
    /* this method deletes an existing directory or sub-directory. It accepts one parameter
     ( 'thePath' of the existing directory/sub-directory) and returns result to the caller */
    public static string deleteDirectory (string thePath)
    {
        try
        {
            Directory.Delete (thePath);    // using 'the file system' delete function
            operationResult = "The directory " + thePath " successfully deleted ...;
        }
        catch (Exception ex)
        {
            operationResult = "Fatal error has occurred ... " + ex.ToString();

        }
        return operationResult;
    } // end of deleteDirectory method
} // end of ManageFileSystem class
```

You can use this static *'**deleteDirectory'*** method in the static *'ManageFileSystem'* class to delete any number of directories/sub-directories/folders in your application. The following example shows how you use the static *'deleteDirectory'* method of the above static *'ManageFileSystem'* class in the *'AppSystemOne'* class:

```
using System;
using System.Windows.Forms;
public class AppSystemOne
{
    private string thePath = " ", operationResult = " ";  // declaring string variables
    public AppSystemOne ()   // constructor - call me to create class instance
    {
        InitializeComponents ();      // initialize all project variables
        deleteExistingFolder ();      // call this method to delete folders
    }
    private void deleteExistingFolder ();
    {
        // delete a root directory called 'asioTech' from the C drive
        thePath = @"C:\asioTech";
        operationResult = ManageFileSystem.deleteExistingDirectory (thePath);
        MessageBox.Show (operationResult);   // display a message after a method call
        // delete a subdirectory called 'forData' from the root directory asioTech
        thePath = @"C:\asioTech\forData";
        operationResult = ManageFileSystem.deleteExistingDirectory (thePath);
        MessageBox.Show (operationResult);   // display a message after a method call
        // delete a subdirectory called forText from the asioTech root directory
        thePath = @"C:\asioTech\forText";
        operationResult = ManageFileSystem.deleteExistingDirectory (thePath);
        MessageBox.Show (operationResult);   // display a message after a method call
        // delete a subdirectory called forImages from the asioTech root directory
        thePath = @"C:\asioTech\forImages";
        operationResult = ManageFileSystem.deleteExistingDirectory (thePath);
        MessageBox.Show (operationResult);   // display a message after a method call
    }
        // rest of  AppSystemOne class members here ....
} // end of AppSystemOne class
```

Under normal circumstances as an applications programmer in an organization, you won't bother with the file system because this is usually done by the systems administration department. But, if you decide to develop an application to sell or to distribute, then your system should be able to dynamically request a space on the user's disk from the operating system so that you can create and organize your files to use in your application.Therefore, you must know how your program can handle the *'File System'*.

WHAT HAVE YOU LEARNED?

- For an application to provide a useful function it needs data to work with.

- Applications can normally read, write, and manipulate data.

- A directory contains the folders and files that the application is able to work with.

- Unique names must be given to stored data, so that it can be found and differentiated from other data.

- The .NET Framework Class Library has the **'System.IO'** namespace with classes that have several methods to allow an application to dynamically act on the data.

CHAPTER 6

WHAT IS A RELATIONAL DATABASE MANAGEMENT SYSTEM?

A Relational Database Management System is a systems software product developed by systems programmers to create a bridge between computer programs and stored data. These software systems mainly support data definition and manipulation operations in programming and improve on the *'File System'* methodology. This provides a very high-level logical view of data representation on a storage device in the form of a table and comes with a unique built-in language for defining and declaring the database and manipulating the data tables in the database.

The Relational Database Management System can contain several databases, and each database can also contain several tables that hold the actual data. The Relational Database Management System manages all the physical data access functionalities on the storage device on behalf of the programmer. Normally, a database contains one or more related tables. A table contains a set of records and the record contains one or more unique fields/properties that describe the characteristics of the record. Examples of the Relational Database Management System are IBM DB2, Microsoft SQL Server and Sybase. The following structure shows a very simple employee database schema with two tables in 'ABC' organization that uses the Relational Database Management System to manage data access:

EmployeeDatabase

EmployeeProfileTable

empID	UserName	Password	Email	jobTitle	empDept
emp01	Tjake99	temasco#80	aHam@abc.com	CEO	Corporate
emp02	nicoLaugh	pharmDept1	tChen@abc.com	President	Marketing
emp03	whiteCat	linskiFirst_#1	pDem@abc.com	Director	IT Lab

EmployeeDetailsTable

empID	FirstName	MiddleName	LastName	PhoneNumber	Gender
emp01	Alexander	Akwasi	Hamilton	012-789-8762	Male
emp02	Tom	Chen	HoLee	98766546679	Female
emp03	Paapa	Linski	Demetrias	01144095543	Male

Figure 1: Database Schema

View database as a library/directory/folder on the storage device; and a table in the database is like a file in a library/directory/folder as described earlier with the *'File System'* data access approach. In the above structure, *'EmployeeDatabase'* is like an 'EmployeeLibrary' or 'EmployeeDirectory' or 'EmployeeFolder' and the tables *'Employee-ProfileTable'* and *'EmployeeDetailsTable'* are like 'EmployeeProfile' and 'EmployeeDetails' files in either EmployeeLibrary' or 'EmployeeDirectory' or 'EmployeeFolder'. Just like how a library/directory/folder can have several files, a database can have several tables and a table can have several records (as long as they don't exceed the allotted storage capacity). A record in a table can also have several fields/properties/attributes that describe the record. In the above tables the identifiers *'empID'*, *'UserName'*, and *'Gender'* are fields, and there are three records in each table that contain the actual data values. Normally, records can be easily accessed through the unique field(s) of a record, this unique field(s) is called the 'key'. When you build your tables, remember to make the first field of a record the 'unique key', for instance, you can use a Social Security number or e-mail address as the key because there won't be any duplicates of the values of this identifier.

STRUCTURED QUERY LANGUAGE (SQL) STATEMENTS

Relational Database Management Systems come with built-in, high-level, unique languages that the computer programmer must know the syntax of in order to use their services. These unique languages have functionalities that support data definitions and manipulations of the data store for the computer programmer. At the time of writing this book, the most common of these languages is SQL (Structured Query Language). This book won't teach you the complete SQL syntax. To learn more you can refer to any number of books on SQL. The following table shows the basic statements (syntax) of the SQL language and their functionalities:

Statement Name	Purpose

create	The 'create' statement is used to create a new database or a new table in an existing database. It's called a data definition statement. The basic format is as follows:
	
	`CREATE DATABASE 'databaseName'`
	`CREATE TABLE 'tableName'`

drop	The 'drop' statement deletes an existing database or an existing table within a specific existing database. The basic format is as follows:
	
	`DROP DATABASE 'databaseName'`
	`DROP TABLE 'tableName'`

delete	The 'delete' statement is used to delete record(s) from one or more tables in the database based on certain conditions. It's also used to delete all records from a table. The basic format is as follows:
	
	`DELETE FROM 'tableName' WHERE 'fieldName' = 'fieldValue'`
	`DELETE * FROM 'tableName'  // delete all records from table`

insert	The 'insert' statement is used to add a new record to a table. This statement adds the new record at the end of the last record. The basic format is as follows:
	
	`INSERT INTO "tableName (field1, field2,...... fieldN)"`
	`VALUES ('value1', 'value2', ....'valueN')`

update	The 'update' statement is used to make changes to certain fields within a table. The basic format is as follows:
	
	`UPDATE 'tableName'  SET 'fieldName' = 'newValue'`
	`UPDATE 'tableName'  SET 'fieldName = 'newValue' WHERE`
	`                            'fieldName'  == 'someValue'`

select	The 'select' statement is used to read/retrieve records from the database depending on several conditions and criteria. The basic format is as follows: `SELECT 'fieldName1', 'fieldName2' 'fieldNameN' FROM 'tableName'`

C#.NET AND THE MICROSOFT ADO.NET

In computer programming, data access is usually considered a very expensive operation. Efficient data access and processing are made more challenging because local area networks, intranets, and the Internet, all compete for simultaneous access to a single data source. ADO stands for Active Data Objects, and its main purpose of this data access is to create functionalities to disconnect data connections during programming from the data store and operate on it, so that the data store can serve multiple clients in Internet applications to promote efficiency and to reduce data access network traffic problems. Data can be manipulated in the system memory and updates can then be applied to the data store whenever. The ADO.NET developers within the Microsoft .NET research group have created some classes with public properties and methods to make this concept feasible, practical, and very easy to use.

Every programming language that wants to use the services of the Relational Database Management System must provide features to allow all the functionalities of that system. The .NET Framework Class Library developers responsible for the optimization of ADO. NET capabilities have created a catalogue of classes with all the necessary functionalities that make using Relational Database Management Systems with the SQL data sub-language extremely easy. You just need to know the classes and use their public members. As explained in chapter 3, the .NET Framework Class Library has a catalog of predefined classes that are available to all programming languages that target the .NET Framework including C#. The '**System.Data.SqlClient**' namespaces in the .NET Framework Class Library have several classes with public members that make data access with SQL very easy using the SQL Server Relational Database Management System in an application. The following table provides the common classes that you can use to manage the SQL Server Relational Database Management System:

Class Name	Namespace	Purpose
SqlConnection	System.Data.SqlClient	This class has methods/constructors to establish the connection to the SQL Server Database Management System, so that a database can be created. You use this class functionality in your program to have access to the database and all its members/tables. An example is to 'open' and 'close' the database.

Class Name	Namespace	Purpose
SqlCommand	System.Data.SqlClient	The command class has several public properties and methods to support the execution of all SQL statements on the database.
SqlDataReader	System.Data.SqlClient	You use the public class methods to do normal forward reading of records from table(s) in a database that do or don't meet certain conditions.

To see how to use the above classes in an application, let's create a class called *'AppSystemTwo'* to handle all our Relational Database Management System operations using the *'Structured Query Language'* in a Microsoft SQL Server 2008 Express version environment.

```
using System;
using System.Data.SqlClient;
using System.Windows.Forms;
using System.Collections.Generic;
public class AppSystemTwo
{
    private string sqlStmt = " "; // a string variable to be used to contain SQL statements
    private string conSQLExpress = "Server=localhost\\SQLEXPRESS;Integrated" +
    "security=SSPI";
    private string conString = "Server=localhost\\SQLEXPRESS;Integrated security=SSPI;" +
    "database=AsioTechDbase";
    public void AppSystemTwo ()   // call me to create an instance of this class
    {
        CreateDataBase ();   // calling the private 'CreateDataBase' method in this class
        CreateTable ();   // calling the private 'CreateTable' method in this class
        AddRecord ();   // calling the private 'AddRecord' method in this class
        UpdateRecord ();   // calling the private 'UpdateRecord' method in this class
        ReadRecord ();   // calling the private 'ReadRecord' method in this class
        DeleteRecord ();   // calling the private 'DeleteRecord' method in this class
        DeleteTable ();   // calling the private 'DeleteTable' method in this class
        DeleteDataBase ();   // calling the private 'DeleteDataBase' method in this class
    }
// all the above methods declaration here starting with the CreateDataBase method
} // end of AppSystemTwo class
```

The above string, that reads:

```
'Server=localhost\\SQLEXPRESS;Integrated security=SSPI'
```

is assigned to the private string variable *'conSQLExpress'* in the *'AppSystemTwo'* class to create a standard connection protocol, currently used by the Microsoft SQL Server

Express Database Management System to allow databases to be created on users/clients computers (this path locator can always be modified by the service provider). Obviously, in order to create a database, you have to connect to the kind of Database Management System you want to use. The path in the above string will change if the Database Management System (DBMS) is located on a different server somewhere across the globe instead on your personal/local computer.

The above string, that reads:

```
'Server=localhost\\SQLEXPRESS;Integrated security=SSPI; database=AsioTechDbase'
```

is assigned to the string variable *conString* in the *AppSystemTwo* class. This string is a standard connection protocol currently used by the Microsoft SQL Server Express Database Management System to allow tables to be created and data to be manipulated in an existing database within the SQL Server Database Management System. Obviously, in order to use a database, you have to connect to it. The path in the above string will change if the Database Management System is located on a different server somewhere across the globe instead of on your personal/local computer.

Note that the path in the above strings database service locators can always be modified by the service provider (in this case, Microsoft Corporation). Generally, as a programmer in an organization, you won't bother yourself with database connectivity issues, but if you decide to write/create your own software products to sell/distribute, then you will definitely have to worry about data storage connectivity issues.

HOW TO CREATE A DATABASE

Under normal circumstances, as a programmer in an organization, you won't be creating a database.This task is usually the responsibility of the database administration department in the organization. But, when you decide to develop a software product that you want to sell or distribute for whatever reason, then you'll want your application to create a database and all the necessary tables that your application will work with. You use the SQL *CREATE DATABASE* statement to create a new database on a storage device. The following example shows how a program dynamically creates a database using the services of the 'System.Data.SqlClient' namespace:

```
private void CreateDataBase () // this method is called by AppSystemTwo class constructor
{
    sqlStmt = "CREATE DATABASE AsioTechDbase";
    SqlConnection conect = new SqlConnection (conSQLExpress);
    SqlCommand cmd = new SqlCommand (sqlStmt, conect);
    try
    {
        conect.Open ();   // connect to the SQL Server Express DBMS
        cmd.ExecuteNonQuery ();   // invoke the SQL 'CREATE DATABASE' statement
        conect.Dispose ();   // disconnect from the SQL Server Express DBMS
    }
    catch (Exception ex)
    {
        conect.Dispose ();
        MessageBox.Show ("Fatal error has occurred  " + ex.ToString ());
    }
} // end of CreateDataBase method
```

HOW TO CREATE A TABLE

Under normal circumstances, as a programmer in an organization, you won't be creating a table in a database. This task is usually the responsibility of the database administration department in the organization. You'll use the SQL '*CREATE TABLE*' statement to create a new table in an existing database on a storage device. The following example shows how a program dynamically creates a new table in a database using the services of the '*System.Data.SqlClient*' namespace:

```
private void CreateTable () // this method is called by AppSystemTwo class constructor
{
    sqlStmt = "CREATE TABLE UserProfileTable " +
                "(UserName VARCHAR (50) PRIMARY KEY," +
                "UserPswd VARCHAR (50) NOT NULL," +
                "UserEmail VARCHAR (50) NOT NULL," +
                "CreateDate VARCHAR (50))";
    SqlConnection conect = new SqlConnection (conString);
    SqlCommand cmd = new SqlCommand (sqlStmt, conect);
    try
    {
        conect.Open (); // open the database
        cmd.ExecuteNonQuery (); // execute the SQL Create Table statement
        conect.Dispose (); // disconnect from the database and release all resources
    }
    catch (Exception ex)
    {
```

```
        conect.Dispose ();
        MessageBox.Show ("Fatal error has occurred  " + ex.ToString ());
    }
} // end of CreateTable method
```

The *'UserName'* in the above *'CreateTable'* method is the first field in the *'UserProfileTable'*.
The *'VARCHAR (50) PRIMARY KEY'* statement means that the *'UserName'* field can contain
up to 50 characters and is the key in this table. The *'UserPswd VARCHAR (50) NOT NULL'*
and *'UserEmail VARCHAR (50) NOT NULL'* statements are fields that can accept up to
50 characters and the fields can't be empty. The *'CreateDate VARCHAR (50)'* statement
expects up to 50 characters to store the date the table was created, but it can be empty.

HOW TO ADD A NEW RECORD TO A TABLE

As a programmer, most of your data access manipulation using a relational database
will be adding records to the database depending on your data access privileges (usually determined by your project manager). You'll use the SQL *'INSERT INTO'* statement
to add a new record to a table in a database. The following example shows how a
program dynamically adds a new record to the *'UserProfileTable'* table in an existing
database. Under normal circumstances, you'll be gathering the user information from
Windows or internet forms and placing them in variables before you insert the record
into the database.

```
private void AddRecord () // this method is called by AppSystemTwo class constructor
{
    sqlStmt = "INSERT INTO UserProfileTable (UserName, UserPswd, UserEmail) " +
                "VALUES ('Tjake99', 'Temasco#1', 'Tjake@yahoo.com')";
    SqlConnection conect = new SqlConnection (conString);
    SqlCommand cmd = new SqlCommand (sqlStmt, conect);
    try
    {
        conect.Open ();   // open the database to use the 'UserProfileTable'
        cmd.ExecuteNonQuery (); // invoke the SQL 'INSERT' function that adds the record
        conect.Dispose ();   // disconnect from the 'AsioTechDbase' database
    }
    catch (Exception ex)
    {
        conect.Dispose ();
        MessageBox.Show ("Fatal error has occurred  " + ex.ToString ());
    }
} // end of AddRecord method
```

HOW TO UPDATE RECORD(S) IN A TABLE

As a programmer, most of your data access manipulation using a relational database will be adding and updating records to the database depending on your data access privileges (usually determined by your project manager). You'll use the SQL *UPDATE* statement to make changes (i.e. modify, update etc.) to records in a table(s) in a database. The following example shows how a program dynamically updates one specific record in the *UserProfileTable* using the *UserName* key field by changing the e-mail address of the user with user name as *tomas99* to a new e-mail address called *tjake@gmail.com*.

```
private void UpdateRecord () // this method is called by AppSystemTwo class constructor
{
    sqlStmt = "UPDATE UserProfileTable " +
              "SET UserEmail = "tjake@gmail.com" WHERE UserName = "tomas99"";
    SqlConnection conect = new SqlConnection (conString);
    SqlCommand cmd = new SqlCommand (sqlStmt, conect);
    try
    {
        conect.Open ();   // open the database to use the 'UserProfileTable'
        cmd.ExecuteNonQuery ();   // invoke the SQL 'UPDATE' function to update record
        conect.Dispose ();   // disconnect from the 'AsioTechDbase' database
    }
    catch (Exception ex)
    {
        conect.Dispose ();
        MessageBox.Show ("Fatal error has occurred  " + ex.ToString ());
    }
} // end of UpdateRecord method
```

HOW TO READ RECORD(S) IN A TABLE

As a programmer, most of your data access manipulation using a relational database will be reading records from the database. You'll use the SQL *SELECT* statement to read record(s) from a table(s) in a database. The following example shows how a program dynamically reads record(s) from a table in an existing database selecting the e-mail address of all users in an organization's *UserProfileTable* and adding them to a *emailList* object in a Windows application:

```
private void ReadRecord () // this method is called by AppSystemTwo class constructor
{
    sqlStmt = "SELECT UserEmail FROM UserProfileTable";
    SqlConnection conect = new SqlConnection (conString);
    SqlCommand cmd = new SqlCommand (sqlStmt, conect);
    SqlDataReader reader;
```

```
    List<Employees> emailList = new List<Employees> ();
    try
    {
        conect.Open ();
        reader = cmd.ExecuteReader ();
        emailList.Clear ();
        while (reader.Read ())
        {
            emailList.Items.Add (reader["UserEmail"].ToString());
        }
        conect.Dispose ();   // disconnect from the database
    }
    catch (Exception ex)
    {
        conect.Dispose ();
        MessageBox.Show ("Fatal error has occurred " + ex.ToString ());
    }
} // end of ReadRecord method
```

HOW TO DELETE RECORD(S) IN A TABLE

As a programmer working in an organization, most of your data access manipulation using a relational database management system will be reading records from the database. Sometimes you'll want to delete records from a table(s) depending on your data access privileges (usually determined by your project manager). You'll use the SQL *DELETE* statement to delete record(s) from a table(s) in a database. The following example shows how a program dynamically deletes a record from the *'UserProfileTable'*:

```
private void DeleteRecord () // this method is called by AppSystemTwo class constructor
{
    sqlStmt = "DELETE FROM UserProfileTable WHERE UserName = "Tjake99";
    SqlConnection conect = new SqlConnection (conString);
    SqlCommand cmd = new SqlCommand (sqlStmt, conect);
    try
    {
        conect.Open (); // connect to 'AsioTechDbase' database
        cmd.ExecuteNonQuery (); // invoke the SQL 'DELETE' function
        conect.Dispose (); // disconnect from the 'AsioTechDbase' database
    }
    catch (Exception ex)
    {
        conect.Dispose ();
        MessageBox.Show ("Fatal error has occurred  " + ex.ToString ());
    }
} // the end of DeleteRecord method
```

HOW TO DELETE A TABLE

Under normal circumstances, as a programmer in an organization, you won't be deleting a table in a database. This task is usually the responsibility of the database administration department in the organization. But, if you develop your software product for sale, you'll want to dynamically be able to manage all your database activities including deleting tables in your database for whatever reason. You'll use the SQL ***DROP TABLE*** statement to remove a table in a database. The following example shows how a program dynamically deletes a table in an existing database:

```
private void DeleteTable () // this method is called by AppSystemTwo class constructor
{
    sqlStmt = "DROP TABLE UserProfileTable";
    SqlConnection conect = new SqlConnection (conString);
    SqlCommand cmd = new SqlCommand (sqlStmt, conect);
    try
    {
        conect.Open (); // connect to the database to use 'UserProfileTable'
        cmd.ExecuteNonQuery (); // invoke the SQL 'DROP TABLE' function
        conect.Dispose (); // disconnect from the database
    }
    catch (Exception ex)
    {
        conect.Dispose ();
        MessageBox.Show ("Fatal error has occurred " + ex.ToString ());
    }
} // end of DeleteTable method
```

HOW TO DELETE A DATABASE

Under normal circumstances, as a programmer in an organization, you won't be deleting a database. This task is usually the responsibility of the database administration department in the organization. Sometimes in your application, you'll want to delete a database for whatever reason. For instance, if you have developed a new software product to sell, but you want potential customers to use your application free for 30 days. Your application will create a database and all the necessary tables on the customer's computers to let them to use the 30-day, free trial offer. Your application will normally give them the option to purchase your software product or to decline after the trial period. Your application will automatically delete the database and all tables from the computers of all those potential customers who decline after 30-day, free trial. You'll use the SQL *'DROP DATABASE'* statement to delete a database called *'AsioTechDbase'* from the SQL Server database management system. The following example shows how a program dynamically deletes a database:

```
private void DeleteDataBase () // this method is called by AppSystemTwo class constructor
{
    sqlStmt = "DROP DATABASE AsioTechDbase";
    SqlConnection conect = new SqlConnection (conSQLExpress);
    SqlCommand cmd = new SqlCommand (sqlStmt, conect);
    try
    {
        conect.Open ();
        cmd.ExecuteNonQuery ();
        conect.Dispose (); // close the connection and release all resources
    }
    catch (System.Exception ex)
    {
        conect.Dispose ();
        MessageBox.Show ("Fatal error has occurred  " + ex.ToString ());
    }
} // end of DeleteDataBase method
```

WHAT HAVE YOU LEARNED?

- Relational Database Management Systems create a bridge between the application and the data, and allows you to view data as tables.

- Programming languages like C# that target the .NET Framework, come with built-in functionalities in the .NET Framework Class Library that allow you to easily use Relational Database Management Systems.

- A standard connection method is Microsoft SQL Server Express Database Management System, which allows databases to be created on a computer.

- SQL statements are used to manipulate databases and even make changes to them automatically.

PART IV

DIFFERENT KINDS OF
PROGRAMMING

This part explains different types of most common programming. Console programming which replaced the first key-punch/
paper programming method is explained with practical examples.
Windows programming, which is the most common programming
style in most organizations today, is explained with practical
examples. Internet programming, which allows us to surf the
web, is explained with a basic and practical example.

WHAT IS BASIC CONSOLE PROGRAMMING?

Console programming uses operating system functions on a console/screen/terminal and the keyboard environment to create applications that directly interact with the computer via the operating system prompts/command line setup, for instance on the C:\ drive prompt. When the computer was invented, terminals/consoles were used to connect to a mainframe or mini-computers. Terminals used to be called 'Cathode Ray Tube' because the terminal/console didn't have a disc to save files/programs to, since every file/program was saved and managed by the connected device (i.e., mainframe and/or mini computers which have the disc storage device). Terminals/consoles are still being used today to connect to mainframe and mini-computers. But right now, the console/terminal is the screen you see on your personal computer; the only difference is this time your computer has a disc to save files/programs to.

Console programming was the first time computer programming used terminals/consoles connected to mainframe computers. The programmer/user interacts with the computer using the keyboard and the console/terminal. This is purely procedural-oriented programming because the programmer/user doesn't have any means of interrupting the execution process. Since programs are created directly using the operating system and the 'Interpreter', console programming is the best place for a beginner to start to learn programming. This is where you will understand how the computer works and be able to use your program with the operating system. Also, you won't have to bother with the complexities of Window's geometrical concept of using x and y coordinates to create points for functions like 'draw', or dragging user-controls/objects onto a windows form just to decorate it for the user's convenience. Instead, you'll focus on the logical part of your program to solve your intended user's problem.

Console projects create command line applications that create an environment for the programmer/user to directly interact with the operating system using a text-only computer interface with the keyboard and the screen/console/terminal. The operating system uses the 'Interpreter', and not the compiler to convert the text into machine code for execution. Console applications don't support the 'Windows Environment System'.

Now, console programming is considered obsolete, but if you want to understand how the operating system and a program work together, you should consider taking the time to learn console programming. Computer science and software engineering students at colleges and universities, use almost 100% console programming in their programming-oriented courses. Most systems programmers like system administrators, network engineers and software engineers in organizations use console programming to test and fine-tune the internal operations of application systems (especially those working at software research labs like IBM, Microsoft, etc.).

At the time of writing this book, the operating systems with the functionalities and capabilities to support console programming are IBM Mainframe and AS400 series operating systems, Windows Win32 console (using DOS shell), Mac OS X Terminal System, UNIX xterm system and the Linux open-ended terminal/console system. All these operating systems have built-in commands that you can use to create and manage a console application. You must learn the commands if you want to use them. For instance, if you want to list the content from a specific directory/folder in a Windows environment, you key in *'dir directory/folderName'*. On the other hand, if you want to list the content from a specific directory/folder in a UNIX or Linux console environment, you key in *'ls directory/folderName'*. Since Linux seems to be the most popular and easy to use operating system right now, you should consider learning console programming. Linux has a catalog of operating system commands that help the programmer to write *'scripts'* (i.e., a combination of programs, files and operating system commands) to achieve unimaginable programming results with minimal coding effort.

CONSOLE PROGRAMMING USING C#.NET

Microsoft Visual Studio Development Kit and the .NET Framework Class Library allow console applications to be created in the same text editor environment used to create Windows and Internet applications. This approach eliminates the concept of command line editing in console programming, allowing us to create a very simple console application using C# in a Visual Studio Development environment. Let us create a very simple console application that will interact directly with the user by asking them to enter their full name. Then the application will ask the user to enter the names of all the user's friends and display them as a list when the user decides to stop entering friends.

To start developing this application, launch 'Microsoft Visual C# 2010 Express', or whichever version you have installed on your computer, as listed in the 'Systems Requirements' in this book. From the 'Start Page', click on 'New Project .... '. From the 'New Project' page, select Visual C# or C# and choose 'Console Application'. Name your application 'Console-App', then click the 'OK' button. Visual Studio will automatically create a default class called 'Program' with one static method called 'Main' and will resolve all the necessary dependencies (i.e., namespaces and references) needed to create a console application using the .NET Framework Class Library. The following is the default console application development environment:

Figure 1. Default Console Application Development Environment

Rename the *'Program.cs'* in the Solution Explorer window as *'ConsoleDialogue.cs'*, and then change the *'Program'* class name to *'ConsoleDialogue'*. Modify the above program as follows:

```
using System;
using System.Collections.Generic;
using System.Linq;
using System.Text;
namespace ConsoleApp
{
 class ConsoleDialogue
 {
  static void Main(string[ ] args)   // the operating system entry point to run this program
  {
    interact_WithUser ();
  }
  // this method interacts with the user
  private static void interact_WithUser ()
  {
    List<string> friends = new List<string>();
    string readerName = " ", yesNoResponse = " ", friendName = " ";
    string yesNoAnswer = "? - Answer Yes or No:";
  BeGin:
    Console.WriteLine("\n Key in your Full Name, press the Enter key to continue:");
    readerName = Console.ReadLine();
    Console.WriteLine("\n Did you say your Full Name" +
    "is " + readerName + yesNoAnswer);
    yesNoResponse = Console.ReadLine();
    yesNoResponse = check_Response(yesNoResponse);
    if (yesNoResponse == "No")
    {
    goto BeGin;
    }
    Console.WriteLine("\n Good " + readerName + " - Welcome to Console" +
    "Programming using Visual Studio and C#. I'm going to have some" +
    "dialogue with you! You are going to enter the Full Names of your friends " +
    "to be displayed on the console. Ok let's start!");
  EnterFriendName:
    Console.WriteLine("\n Key in a friend's Full Name, press the Enter key:");
    friendName = Console.ReadLine(); // receive a friend name from the console
    Console.WriteLine("\n Did you say your friend's " +
    "Full Name is " + friendName + yesNoAnswer);
    yesNoResponse = Console.ReadLine();
    yesNoResponse = check_Response(yesNoResponse);
```

```csharp
        if (yesNoResponse == "No")
            {
                goto EnterFriendName;
            }
        friends.Add(friendName);      // add a friend to the friend list
        Console.WriteLine("\n Hi there " + readerName + " - do you want to enter" +
        "another friend's name?  " + yesNoAnswer);
        yesNoResponse = Console.ReadLine();
        yesNoResponse = check_Response(yesNoResponse);
        if (yesNoResponse == "Yes")
            goto EnterFriendName;
        else
            display_Friends(friends, readerName);
    }
    // this method checks for user response
    private static string check_Response (string response)
    {
        while ((response != "Yes") & (response != "No"))
        {
            Console.WriteLine("\n Wrong response. Your response must be" +
            "Yes or No: The C# language is a case sensitive language " +
            "(i.e. 'Yes' is different  from 'yes' and 'No' is different from 'no'!) " +
            "- try again");
            response = Console.ReadLine();
        }
        return response;
    }
    // this method displays all friends on the console
    private static string display_Friends(List<string> friends, string theUser)
    {
        Console.WriteLine("The following are your friends:\n");
        foreach (string friend in friends)
        {
            Console.WriteLine("\t " + friend);
        }
        Console.WriteLine("\nHi there " + theUser + " - have a nice day." +
        "I hope to see you again!");
        Console.ReadLine();
        return " ";
    }
  } // end of ConsoleDialogue class
} // end of ConsoleApp namespace
```

Choose 'Debug' from the menu bar and select 'Start Debugging' to compile and run/execute the above program, you will see the following environment after you have interacted with all the instructions in the program:

Figure 2. A Console Application

WHAT HAVE YOU LEARNED?

- Console programming allows you to directly interact with the operating system by entering lines of code.

- Even though console programming is considered obsolete, it's very useful for learning how the application and operating system interact.

- A console application can be created very easily using the .NET Framework Class Library.

CHAPTER 8

WHAT IS BASIC WINDOWS PROGRAMMING?

Windows programming creates application systems that allow the user maximum control over the application's behavior in a Windows environment instead of using the computer operating system command lines or prompts as explained in console programming. Windows programming is a very big improvement on console programming. Program execution isn't sequential, because it can be interrupted by the user.

Windows programming is completely object-oriented programming, because it uses instances of classes (objects) to control the application system's behavior. These are sometimes called user-friendly or event-driven applications. The term 'window' is a user-defined data type 'class' called 'window' with properties and methods like, 'Title', 'Maximize, 'Minimize', 'Hide', 'Close' and other standard user-interface elements. So, the 'window' form that a software development kit automatically creates when you start to develop a Windows application is an object that's an instance of the window 'class'. A main window can contain another window as a child window. For instance, you can create a dialogue window that requires the user to respond before a given action can be performed. In this chapter, you'll learn how to use dialogue windows.

Windows applications are usually developed in a software development kit environment with a 'Tool Box' that contains user-interface controls. The windows object acts as a container for other objects in the 'Tool Box' such as: 'button', 'label', 'textbox', 'combobox', 'image', 'audio', 'video', etc. The objects you drag and drop to the windows form are also instances of 'classes' and inherit all the public and protected members of their classes. Windows programming uses the events/functions of the objects from the 'Tool Box' to manage the behavior of the application. For instance, a mouse or a finger 'click' event on a 'submit' button uses 'click event handler' to instruct the application to send the content of a form to a database or to another function in the application, or to another function in a different application. A 'cancel' event uses a 'cancel event handler' to terminate an operation. Event handlers in Windows programming are functions that perform a specific task for an object and are fully controlled by the user of the application.

Windows programming is usually developed to target desktop, laptop, and tablet devices. Most organizations use Windows applications because they can be controlled and managed by the organization. Large organizations usually use local area network (LAN) for their computer operations. That's because there will only be one desktop/laptop acting as the server for all the operations in the business, but with several desktops/laptops/tablets connected to it. Nobody can have access to the organization's information, unless authorized (usually by a systems administrator or the owner of the organization). This environment is usually called a 'client/server' application system environment.

As an aspiring Computer Programmer/Software Developer, most of the applications you develop will be Windows applications, because that's what most organizations use to manage their business operations. This chapter provides a practical case study of a very basic Windows Application System development process using Microsoft Visual Studio Software Development Kit with the C# programming language.

WINDOWS PROGRAMMING USING C#.NET

At the time of writing this book, one of the best Software Development Environment to use to create professional, world-class enterprise Windows Software Product Solutions for an organization, for personal use or to sell/distribute, is the Microsoft Visual Studio Development tool with the .NET Framework and the C# programming language. This is because Windows programming is object-oriented programming and the C# programming language is a complete object-oriented programming language with an unimaginably large amount of predefined class/objects functions that support the .NET Framework Class Library. Because of the built-in artificial intelligence services provided by Visual

Studio and .NET Framework Class Library, you can create a complete Windows application with minimal coding effort once you understand the meaning of the user-defined data type 'class' and its functionalities, which we discussed in chapter 3. Note that you can always build your Windows Application Systems in any Software Development Kit environment with the programming language of your choice.

WINDOWS FORMS, TOOLBOX, PROPERTIES, EVENTS AND EVENT HANDLERS

Visual Studio provides all the parts needed to create an enterprise Windows Application System. The 'Windows Forms' that acts as a container for user-interface controls, such as: 'button', 'textbox', 'label' etc. are all instances of a Windows Form 'class' (i.e., object). The 'Toolbox' contains user-interface controls and the controls you drag and drop to a Windows Form. These are also instances of the user-control 'classes' (i.e., objects).

Since Windows Forms and the Toolbox User-Interface Controls are 'classes', you can use the properties of the objects to describe the characteristics of the objects on the Windows Form. You also use events like 'click' and 'mousehover', and respond to the event by implementing event handlers/methods (i.e., methods/functions to subscribe to the notification of the events) as the user reacts to the object on the form.

SAMPLE WINDOWS APPLICATION SYSTEM DEVELOPMENT PROCESS

In this project, you'll develop a very simple Windows software product that targets employee profile management that you can sell to organizations. The application allows any number of new employees to 'Sign Up' simultaneously when hired. Existing employees can also 'Sign In' simultaneously anytime to update/manage their profiles. The system administrator is the only one who has the authorization to view all employee profiles, as well as delete an employee at the management's request. The application doesn't allow the system administrator to update any employee's profile. The application system has the following basic functionalities:

- Organization/Client Registration Process
- Dynamic Database and Tables Creation
- New Employee Information Profile Creation

- Existing Employee Information Management
- System Administrator's All Employees Profile Management

In this application, the moment you purchase our product, you're ready to go. Under normal circumstances, you'll be given a trial period; but this application assumes that you have decided to purchase our product and are ready to install it. Now, as an aspiring programmer, you'll be able to create this type of application when you finish reading this book.

APPLICATION SYSTEM ANALYSIS AND DESIGN

As explained in chapter 4, you should always analyze and design a target application before development. So, in this system, you've decided to use the SQL database management system as the data store for the employees of the potential organization. Since you're developing this Application System using the tools from Visual Studio, the .NET Framework and C# programming language, our analysis and design process came up with the following 'classes/program parts' to accomplish our target/goal:

- MiscClass.cs – (a static class to handle miscellaneous operations)
- InstallForm.cs – (the client/organization profile registration environment)
- MainForm.cs – (the first window to see after company registration and everyday)
- SignInForm.cs – (the everyday SignUp/SignIn for new and existing employees)
- ProfileForm.cs – (the whenever employee profile management environment)
- StartUp.cs – (the default operating system point of entry to run our application)

To start developing this software product, launch the 'Microsoft Visual C# 2010 Express' or whichever version you have installed on your computer. From the 'Start Page', select 'New Project ...'. From the 'New Project' page, select Visual C# from the installed templates and choose Windows Form Application. Name your application 'WindowsApp', then click the 'OK' button. Visual Studio automatically provides two default classes (i.e., programs) for you (i.e., Form1.cs and Program.cs). If you don't see the 'Solution Explorer' window, click on it on the menu bar.

Now, let's add the new class that's going to be used to handle all miscellaneous operations in our application. Click on 'Project' item on the menu bar and select the 'Add Class …' option. From the 'New Item' window, select Visual C# and choose the 'Class' option. Name the class 'MiscClass' and click the 'Add' button. Visual Studio will display the following empty default class environment:

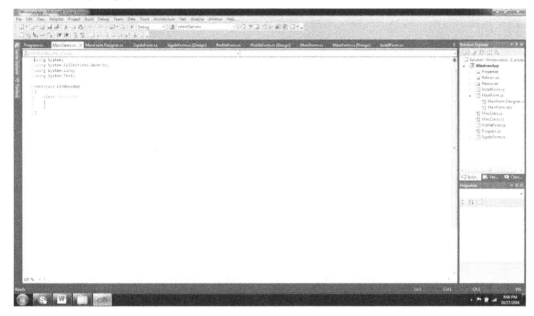

Figure 1. Empty Default Class

MISCCLASS.CS

Since you need the database to store both the potential organization and employee profiles in this application, you'll do some coding in this class first. Let's change the class to static (i.e., methods/functions from other classes can use members of this class without creating an instance of this class (objects) as explained in chapter 3). This class is used to create databases and tables, as well as provide 'public' common variables to be used throughout the whole application. Note that in programming, there's no specific methodology or standard way of expressing the logical solution to a problem, because different people solve the same problem differently. The following is the modified program for the 'MiscClass' class shown in figure 1:

```csharp
using System;
using System.Collections.Generic;
using System.Linq;
using System.Text;
using System.Data.SqlClient;
namespace WindowsApp
{
 static class MiscClass
 {
    private static string errorMsg = " ", sqlStmt = " ";
    public static string sysadmin = "System Administrator", cancelButton = "Cancel";
    public static string deleteButton = "Delete";
    public static string resetButton = "Reset", goButton = "Go >>";
    public static string updateButton = "Update";
    public static string entryMsg = "Enter User Name and Password, Click Sign In";
    public static string sysVersion = "empSys (1.1)";
    public static string compSlogan = "......building bridges of research across " +
    "the globe......";
    private static string dbmsConnect = "Server=localhost\\SQLEXPRESS;Integrated"+
    "security=SSPI";
    public static string dbaseConnect = "Server=localhost\\SQLEXPRESS;Integrated"+
    "security=SSPI; database=SkipCollegeDbase";
    public static string ManageDatabase()
    {
        CreateDatabase();
        if (errorMsg != " ")
        return errorMsg;
        CreateCompProfileTable();
        if (errorMsg != " ")
        return errorMsg;
        CreateEmpProfileTable();
        return errorMsg;
    }
    // this method uses SQL to create a database
    private static void CreateDatabase() // this private method is being called
    by ManageDatabase method
    {
        sqlStmt = "CREATE DATABASE SkipCollegeDbase";
        SqlConnection conect = new SqlConnection(dbmsConnect);
        SqlCommand cmd = new SqlCommand(sqlStmt, conect);
        try
        {
            conect.Open();
            cmd.ExecuteNonQuery();
            conect.Dispose();
        }
```

```
        catch (Exception ex)
        {
            errorMsg = "Problem Creating Database - " + ex.ToString();
            conect.Dispose();
        }
    }
}
```
// **this method uses SQL to create a Company Profile table**
```
    private static void CreateCompProfileTable()    // this private method is being called by
ManageDatabase method
    {
        sqlStmt = "CREATE TABLE CompProfileTable (CompanyName VARCHAR(50)" +
        "PRIMARY KEY," + "StreetAddress VARCHAR(50) NOT NULL," +
        "CityName VARCHAR(50) NOT NULL, StateName VARCHAR(50) NOT NULL, " +
        "ZipCode VARCHAR(50) NOT NULL, CountryName VARCHAR(50) NOT NULL, " +
        "CompanyPhone VARCHAR(50) NOT NULL, CompanyWebSite VARCHAR(50), " +
        "InstallerStatus VARCHAR(50), CreatedBy VARCHAR(100) NOT NULL, " +
        "CreateDate VARCHAR(50))";
        SqlConnection conect = new SqlConnection(dbaseConnect);
        SqlCommand cmd = new SqlCommand(sqlStmt, conect);
        try
        {
            conect.Open();
            cmd.ExecuteNonQuery();
            conect.Dispose();
        }
        catch (System.Exception ex)
        {
            errorMsg = "Problem Creating Company Profile Table - " + ex.ToString();
            conect.Dispose();
        }
    }
```
// **this method uses SQL to create Employee Profile table**
```
    private static void CreateEmpProfileTable()      // this private method is being called
by ManageDatabase method
    {
        sqlStmt = "CREATE TABLE EmpProfileTable (UserName VARCHAR(50) " +
        "PRIMARY KEY, UserPswd VARCHAR(50) NOT NULL, FirstName VARCHAR(50) " +
        "NOT NULL, MiddleName VARCHAR(50), LastName VARCHAR(50) NOT NULL, " +
        "ContactPhone VARCHAR(50) NOT NULL, Gender VARCHAR(10) NOT NULL, " +
        "EmailAddress VARCHAR(50), BirthDate VARCHAR(50) NOT NULL, " +
        "EmergencyPhone VARCHAR(50), UserStatus VARCHAR(50) NOT NULL, " +
        "Remarks TEXT, EmpProfile VARCHAR(200), CreateDate VARCHAR(50))";
        SqlConnection conect = new SqlConnection(dbaseConnect);
        SqlCommand cmd = new SqlCommand(sqlStmt, conect);
        try
        {
```

```
            conect.Open();
                cmd.ExecuteNonQuery();
                conect.Dispose();
        }
        catch (System.Exception ex)
        {
                errorMsg = "Problem Creating Employee Profile Table - " + ex.ToString();
                conect.Dispose();
        }
    }
  } // end of MiscClass class
} // end of namespace WindowsApp
```

INSTALLFORM.CS [DESIGN]

Let's rename the default windows 'Form1.cs' in the Solution Explorer to 'InstallForm.cs'. Resize the form to meet your needs, then click on 'Toolbox' from the menu bar and you'll see the following environment:

Figure 2. InstallForm.cs [Design] – Empty Windows Form with Toolbox, Solution Explorer and Property Windows

INSTALLFORM.CS [DESIGN]' AND OTHER OBJECTS/UI CONTROLS

Let's drag picture, label, textbox and button objects from the Toolbox and place them on the 'InstallForm'. Now click/focus on the left picture object, and click the Image property in the property window, and select the picture you like. If you don't already have images, click on the 'Import' button and select the picture you want from the picture gallery on your computer. You'll see the following environment:

Figure 3. InstallForm.cs [Design] – Importing Image Dialogue Box to Fill Left Picture Object

When you click the 'OK' button, you'll see the following window:

Figure 4. InstallForm.cs [Design] – Left Picture Object Filled After Importing Image from Image Gallery

Now click/focus on the right picture, and click on the Image property and select another picture from your picture gallery. You'll see the following environment:

Figure 5. InstallForm.cs [Design] – Importing Image from the Image Gallery to Fill Right Picture Object

If you've finished importing the image from your gallery, then click the 'OK' button and you'll see the following environment with both images on 'InstallForm':

Figure 6. InstallForm.cs [Design] – After Importing Images to Fill Two 'Picture' Objects on a Window Form

INSTALLFORM.CS [DESIGN]' PROPERTY SETTINGS

As explained in chapter 3, the 'class' user-defined data type includes members such as 'Property' that describes the characteristics of the 'class'; and since you already know that 'Window' is also a class and our 'InstallForm' is an instance of the Windows Form class, then you can manage this form to meet our needs through the 'Property' settings in the property window. In this project, you want to set the 'InstallForm' background color property to black. Let's drag and drop some 'textbox' and 'button' objects onto the 'InstallForm'. Now, let's set the labels text property to meaningfull identifiers like 'Company Name', 'Street Address', etc., for the client registration environment. After these properties are set the 'InstallForm'.cs [Design] environment will look like this:

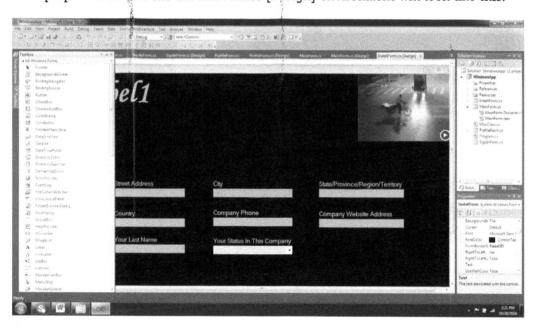

Figure 7. InstallForm.cs [Design] with Labels, Textbox and Buttons

Now click 'Debug' on the menu bar, and select 'Start Debugging', you'll see the following environment with the sample organization registration information:

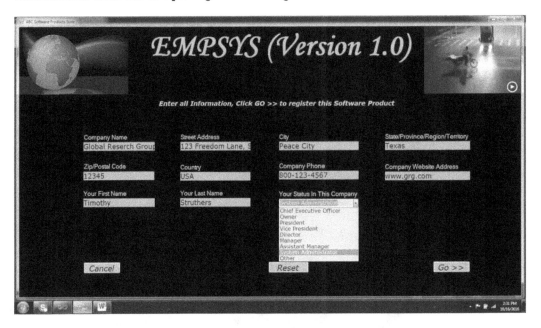

Figure 8. InstallForm Window - Client Profile Registration Environment

The following is the source code (i.e., the program) for the 'InstallForm.cs' window. To see this code, click 'View' on the menu bar and select 'Code'.

```
using System;
using System.Collections.Generic;
using System.ComponentModel;
using System.Data;
using System.Data.SqlClient;
using System.Drawing;
using System.Linq;
using System.Text;
using System.Windows.Forms;    // Form class is in this namespace
namespace WindowsApp
{
  public partial class InstallForm : Form // InstallForm class inherits Form class
  {
      string sqlStmt = " ", errorMsg = " ";
      string instMsg = "Enter all Information, Click GO >> to register this Software Product";
      public InstallForm()     // the class constructor
```

```csharp
{
    InitializeComponent();        // this method is in InstallForm.Designer.cs
    this.Text = "ABC Software Products Suite";
    compNameLabel.Text = "EMPSYS (Version 1.0)";
    userInstructLabel.Text = instMsg;
    cancelButton.Text = MiscClass.cancelButton;
    resetButton.Text = MiscClass.resetButton;
    goButton.Text = MiscClass.goButton;
    errorMsg = MiscClass.ManageDatabase();
    if (errorMsg != " ")
        return;
    init_Stuff();
}
// this method/function initializes variables
private void init_Stuff()
{
    cnameTxt.Text = " ";
    addressTxt.Text = " ";
    cityTxt.Text = " ";
    stateTxt.Text = " ";
    zipTxt.Text = " ";
    countryTxt.Text = " ";
    cphoneTxt.Text = " ";
    siteTxt.Text = " ";
    fnameTxt.Text = " ";
    lnameTxt.Text = " ";
}
// the cancel button event handler
private void cancelButton_Click(object sender, EventArgs e)
{
    this.Close();
}
// the reset button event handler
private void resetButton_Click(object sender, EventArgs e)
{
    init_Stuff();
}
// the go button event handler
private void goButton_Click(object sender, EventArgs e)
{
    register_Company();
    if (errorMsg != " ")
    {
        MessageBox.Show(errorMsg);
        return;
    }
```

```
      this.Hide();
      MainForm mform = new MainForm();      // creating an instance/object of the Main-
Form class
      mform.ShowDialog();
   }

   // this method registers the client information in a database
   private void register_Company()
   {
     string empProfile = (fnameTxt.Text + " " + lnameTxt.Text);
     sqlStmt = "INSERT INTO CompProfileTable (CompanyName, StreetAddress," +
     "CityName, StateName, ZipCode, CountryName, CompanyPhone, " +
     "CompanyWebSite, InstallerStatus, CreatedBy, CreateDate)" +
     "VALUES (@CompanyName, @StreetAddress, @CityName, @StateName, " +
     "@ZipCode, @CountryName, @CompanyPhone, @CompanyWebSite, " +
     "@InstallerStatus, @CreatedBy, @CreateDate)";
     SqlConnection conect = new SqlConnection(MiscClass.dbaseConnect);
     SqlCommand cmd = new SqlCommand(sqlStmt, conect);
     cmd.Parameters.Add("@CompanyName", SqlDbType.VarChar, 50).Value
      = cnameTxt.Text;
     cmd.Parameters.Add("@StreetAddress", SqlDbType.VarChar, 50).Value
      = addressTxt.Text;
     cmd.Parameters.Add("@CityName", SqlDbType.VarChar, 50).Value = cityTxt.Text;
     cmd.Parameters.Add("@StateName", SqlDbType.VarChar, 50).Value = stateTxt.Text;
     cmd.Parameters.Add("@ZipCode", SqlDbType.VarChar, 50).Value = zipTxt.Text;
     cmd.Parameters.Add("@CountryName", SqlDbType.VarChar, 50).Value
      = countryTxt.Text;
     cmd.Parameters.Add("@CompanyPhone", SqlDbType.VarChar, 50).Value
      = cphoneTxt.Text;
     cmd.Parameters.Add("@CompanyWebSite", SqlDbType.VarChar, 50).Value
      = siteTxt.Text;
     cmd.Parameters.Add("@InstallerStatus", SqlDbType.VarChar, 50).Value
      = empStatusList.Text;
     cmd.Parameters.Add("@CreatedBy", SqlDbType.VarChar, 100).Value = empProfile;
     cmd.Parameters.Add("@CreateDate", SqlDbType.VarChar, 50).Value
      = DateTime.Now.ToString();
     try
     {
        conect.Open();
        cmd.ExecuteNonQuery();
        conect.Dispose();
     }
     catch (Exception ex)
     {
        conect.Dispose();
        errorMsg = "Error Adding Company Record " + ex.ToString();
     }
   }
```

```
}  // end of InstallForm class
}  // end WindowsApp namespace
```

In accordance with good design practices, you want all the Windows Forms (i.e., the User-Interface) in this application to be the same size, and have the same background color, look, and feel as the 'InstallForm.cs'. Therefore, let's copy 'InstallForm.cs' and paste it into 'MainForm.cs', 'SignInForm.cs', and 'ProfileForm.cs'.

MAINFORM.CS [DESIGN]

Since you copied 'InstallForm.cs' and renamed it 'MainForm.cs', let's delete all the User-Interface Control/Objects that you don't want on 'MainForm' and drag and drop the User-Interface Control/Objects from the 'Toolbox' that you want onto this Form. Let's drag and drop some 'labels' and a 'button' unto the 'MainForm' design Form. The 'Main-Form.cs [Design]' environment will look like this after the updates:

Figure 9. MainForm.cs [Design] – Client Everyday First Window Design Environment

Now, when you click the Go >> button on the 'InstallForm' window after entering the client information, you'll see the following environment with the organization information that the system administrator or company owner entered during the client registration process on the 'InstallForm' environment:

Figure 10. MainForm Window – Client First Everyday Window When Employees Turn on Their Computers

The following is the source code (i.e., program) for 'MainForm.cs' window. To see this code, click 'View' on the menu bar and select 'Code'.

```
using System;
using System.Collections.Generic;
using System.ComponentModel;
using System.Data;
using System.Data.SqlClient;
using System.Drawing;
using System.Linq;
using System.Text;
using System.Windows.Forms;
namespace WindowsApp
{
  public partial class MainForm : Form      // MainForm class inherits Form class
  {
      string errorMsg = " ", city = " ", state = " ", zip = " ", country = " ";
      public MainForm()   // the class constructor
```

```csharp
{
    InitializeComponent();          // this method is in MainForm.Designer.cs class
    compSloganLabel.Text = MiscClass.compSlogan;
    load_CompanyInfo();
    if (errorMsg != " ")
    {
        MessageBox.Show(errorMsg);
        return;
    }
    compNameLabel.Text = regCompLabel.Text;
    cityZipCountryLabel.Text = (city + ", " + state + " " + zip + " " + country);
}
// this method loads the company information into variables
private void load_CompanyInfo()
{
    string sqlStmt = "SELECT CompanyName, StreetAddress, CityName, " +
    "StateName, ZipCode, CountryName, CompanyPhone, " +
    "CompanyWebSite FROM CompProfileTable";
    SqlConnection conect = new SqlConnection(MiscClass.dbaseConnect);
    SqlCommand cmd = new SqlCommand(sqlStmt, conect);
    SqlDataReader reader;
    try
    {
        conect.Open();
        reader = cmd.ExecuteReader();
        if (reader.Read())
        {
            regCompLabel.Text = reader["CompanyName"].ToString();
            streetAddressLabel.Text = reader["StreetAddress"].ToString();
            city = reader["CityName"].ToString();
            state = reader["StateName"].ToString();
            zip = reader["ZipCode"].ToString();
            country = reader["CountryName"].ToString();
            cphoneLabel.Text = "Telephone: " + reader["CompanyPhone"].ToString();
            siteLabel.Text = "Website: " + reader["CompanyWebSite"].ToString();
        }
        conect.Dispose();
    }
    catch (Exception ex)
    {
        conect.Dispose();
        errorMsg = "Error reading CompProfileTable. " + ex.ToString();
    }
}
// this method is the go button click event handler
private void goButton_Click(object sender, EventArgs e)
```

```
    {
        SignInForm signin = new SignInForm(compNameLabel.Text);     // creating instance
of SignInForm
        signin.ShowDialog();
    }
    // this method is the website label click event handler
    private void siteLabel_Click(object sender, EventArgs e)
    {
        string tryagain = "This Website is currently under construction – try next time!";
        MessageBox.Show(tryagain, compNameLabel.Text, MessageBoxButtons.OK, +
        MessageBoxIcon.Information);
    }
} // end of MainForm class
} // end of namespace WindowsApp
```

SIGNINFORM.CS [DESIGN]

Since you copied 'InstallForm' and renamed it 'SignInForm', let's delete all the User-Interface Control/Objects that you don't want on this form, and drag and drop the User-Interface Control/Objects from the 'Toolbox' that you do want on this form. First, let's drag and drop 'textbox', 'radiobutton', 'button', etc., onto our design environment. The following will be the 'SignInForm.cs [Design]' environment after this form updates:

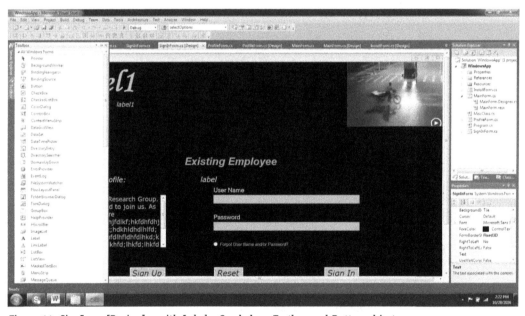

Figure 11. SignIn.cs [Design] – with Labels, Combobox, Textbox and Button objects

Now, click 'Debug' on the menu bar and select 'Start Debugging' to compile/run/test the above Window/Form. You'll see the following window with the 'New Employee', 'Existing Employee', 'Sign Up', and 'Sign In' environments:

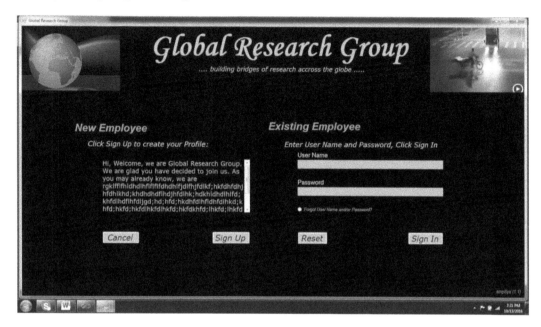

Figure 12. SignIn.cs [Design] – Employee Sign-In and Sign-Up Design Environment

The following is the source code (i.e., program) for 'SignInForm.cs'. To see this code, click 'View' on the menu bar and select 'Code'.

```
using System;
using System.Collections.Generic;
using System.ComponentModel;
using System.Data;
using System.Data.SqlClient;
using System.Drawing;
using System.Linq;
using System.Text;
using System.Windows.Forms;
namespace WindowsApp
{
  public partial class SignInForm : Form      // SignInForm class inherits the Form class
  {
      string cname = " ", userName = " ", userStatus = " ", sqlStmt = " ", errorMsg = " ";
      string invalidMsg = "Invalid User Name and/or Password - try again!";
```

```csharp
public SignInForm()       // the base constructor
{
    Initialize_Component();
}
private void Initialize_Component()
{
    InitializeComponent();     // this method is in SignInForm.Designer.cs class
    this.Text = cname;
    compNameLabel.Text = cname;
    compSloganLabel.Text = MiscClass.compSlogan;
    versionName.Text = MiscClass.sysVersion;
    signInLabel.Text = MiscClass.entryMsg;
    init_Fields();
}
public SignInForm(string compName)     // overloaded constructor
{
    cname = compName;
    Initialize_Component();
}
private void init_Fields()
{
    userNameTxt.Text = " ";
    pswdTxt.Text = " ";
}
// this is the SignUp button event handler
private void signUpButton_Click(object sender, EventArgs e)
{
    userName = " ";
    userStatus = " ";
    show_ProfileForm();
}
private void show_ProfileForm()
{
    this.Hide();
    ProfileForm pform = new ProfileForm(userName, userStatus, cname);
    pform.ShowDialog();
}
// this is the Reset button event handler
private void resetButton_Click(object sender, EventArgs e)
{
    init_Fields();
}
// this is the go button event handler
private void goButton_Click(object sender, EventArgs e)
```

```
{
    if ((userNameTxt.Text == "") || (pswdTxt.Text == ""))
    {
        MessageBox.Show(MiscClass.entryMsg, cname, MessageBoxButtons.OK,
        MessageBoxIcon.Exclamation);
        return;
    }
    verify_SignInInfo();
    if (errorMsg == "n")
    {
        MessageBox.Show(invalidMsg, cname, MessageBoxButtons.OK,
        MessageBoxIcon.Exclamation);
        return;
    }
    if (errorMsg == " ")
        show_ProfileForm();
    else
        MessageBox.Show(errorMsg, cname, MessageBoxButtons.OK,
        MessageBoxIcon.Exclamation);
}
// this method verifies user name and password
private void verify_SignInInfo()
{
    errorMsg = " ";
    sqlStmt = "SELECT UserName, UserPswd, UserStatus FROM EmpProfileTable " +
            "WHERE UserName = '" + userNameTxt.Text + "' AND UserPswd = '" +
             pswdTxt.Text + "'";
    SqlConnection conect = new SqlConnection(MiscClass.dbaseConnect);
    SqlCommand cmd = new SqlCommand(sqlStmt, conect);
    SqlDataReader reader;
    try
    {
        conect.Open();
        reader = cmd.ExecuteReader();
        if (reader.Read())
        {
            userName = reader["UserName"].ToString();
            userStatus = reader["UserStatus"].ToString();
        }
        else
        {
            errorMsg = "n";
        }
        conect.Dispose();
```

```
            return;
        }
        catch (Exception ex)
        {
            conect.Dispose();
            errorMsg = "Error Reading EmpProfileTable. " + ex.ToString();
        }
    }
    // this is the Cancel button event handler
    private void cancelButton_Click(object sender, EventArgs e)
    {
        this.Close();
    }
  } // end of SignInForm class
} // end of WindowsApp namespace
```

PROFILEFORM.CS [DESIGN]

Since you copied 'InstallForm' and renamed it 'ProfileForm', let's delete all the User-Interface Controls/Objects that you don't want on this form, and drag and drop the User-Interface Controls/Objects from the 'Toolbox' that you do want. So, let's drag and drop 'label', 'listbox', 'textbox', 'combobox', 'button', etc., onto our design environment. The 'ProfileForm.cs [Design]' environment will be as follows after the updates:

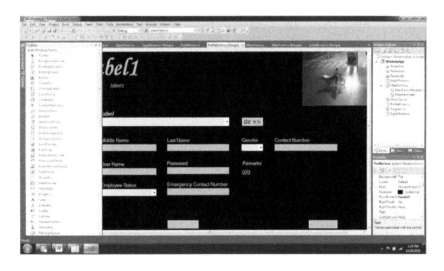

Figure 13. ProfileForm.cs [Design] – with Labels, Combobox, Textbox and Button objects

If you're a new employee and you click the 'Sign Up' button on the 'SignInForm' window, you'll see the following window after you've entered your information.

Figure 14. ProfileForm Window – New Employee Profile Setup

If you're an existing employee and you sign in with the wrong user name and/or wrong password, you'll see the following window with a dialogue window asking you to enter the correct user name and/or password:

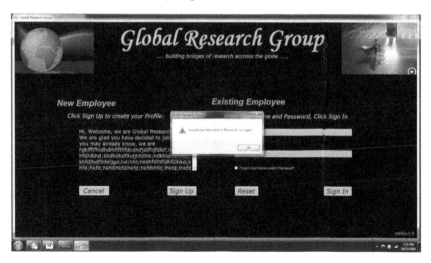

Figure 15. SignInForm Window – Invalid User Name and/or Password During Existing Employee Sign-In Process

If you're an existing employee and you sign in with valid user name and password to update your profile, you'll see the following window:

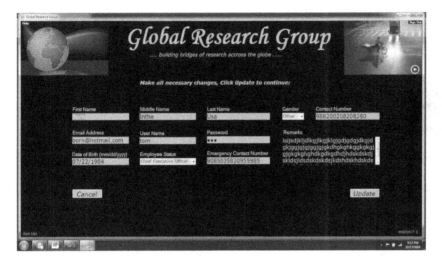

Figure 16. ProfileForm Window – Existing Employee Profile Update Environment

If you're the system administrator and you 'Sign In', you'll see the following window to view the list of all employees. The system allows only the system administrator to view and delete an employee profile for any reason.

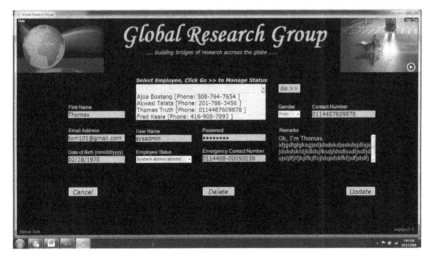

Figure 17. ProfileForm Window – System Administrator All Employees Profile View and Delete Environment

The following is the source code (i.e., program) for 'ProfileForm.cs'. To view this code, click 'View' on the menu bar and select 'Code'.

```
using System;
using System.Collections.Generic;
using System.ComponentModel;
using System.Data;
using System.Data.SqlClient;
using System.Drawing;
using System.Linq;
using System.Text;
using System.Windows.Forms;
namespace WindowsApp
{
  public partial class ProfileForm : Form        // ProfileForm class inherits Form class
  {
      int totalEmployees = 0;
      string sqlStmt = " ", endresult = " ", UserName = " ", UserStatus = " ";
      string instMsg = "Make all necessary changes, Click Update to continue:";
      public ProfileForm()     // Base constructor
      {
          Initialize_Component();
      }
      private void Initialize_Component()
      {
          InitializeComponent();
          compSloganLabel.Text = MiscClass.compSlogan;
          versionName.Text = MiscClass.sysVersion;
          init_Stuff();
      }
      private void init_Stuff()
      {
          fnameTxt.Text = " ";
          mnameTxt.Text = " ";
          lnameTxt.Text = " ";
          phoneTxt.Text = " ";
          emailTxt.Text = " ";
          userNameTxt.Text = " ";
          pswdTxt.Text = " ";
          dobTxt.Text = " ";
          emergencyPhoneTxt.Text = " ";
          remarksTxt.Text = " ";
      }
      // this is overloaded constructor with three parameters
```

```
public ProfileForm(string userName, string userStatus, string compName)
{
    Initialize_Component();
    UserName = userName;
    UserStatus = userStatus;
    this.Text = compName;
    compNameLabel.Text = compName;
    empList.Visible = false;
    selectButton.Visible = false;
    if (UserStatus == MiscClass.sysadmin)
    {
        userInstructLabel.Text = instMsg;
        deleteResetButton.Text = MiscClass.deleteButton;
        goButton.Text = MiscClass.updateButton;
        load_Employees();
        if (endresult != "")
        {
            MessageBox.Show(endresult);
            return;
        }
        if (totalEmployees != 0)
        {
            userInstructLabel.Text = "Select Employee, Click Go >> to Manage Status";
            empList.Visible = true;
            selectButton.Visible = true;
        }
    }
    if (UserName == " ")
    {
        userInstructLabel.Text = "Enter all applicable information, "+
        "Click Go >> to save:";
        empList.Visible = false;
        deleteResetButton.Text = MiscClass.resetButton;
        goButton.Text = MiscClass.goButton;
        currentUserLabel.Text = "Current User: New Employee";
    }
    if ((UserName != " ") && (UserStatus != MiscClass.sysadmin))
    {
        userInstructLabel.Text = instMsg;
        deleteResetButton.Visible = false;
        goButton.Text = MiscClass.updateButton;
    }
    if (UserName != " ")
    {
```

```
        get_EmployeeInfo();
        if (endresult != " ")
            MessageBox.Show(endresult);
        else
            currentUserLabel.Text = (fnameTxt.Text + " " + lnameTxt.Text);
    }
}
// this method loads all employees into a list for the system administrator
private void load_Employees()
{
    endresult = " ";
    sqlStmt = "SELECT EmpProfile FROM EmpProfileTable";
    SqlConnection conect = new SqlConnection(MiscClass.dbaseConnect);
    SqlCommand cmd = new SqlCommand(sqlStmt, conect);
    SqlDataReader reader;
    try
    {
        empList.Items.Clear();
        conect.Open();
        reader = cmd.ExecuteReader();
        while (reader.Read())
        {
            empList.Items.Add(reader["EmpProfile"].ToString());
            totalEmployees = totalEmployees + 1;
        }
        conect.Dispose();
    }
    catch (Exception ex)
    {
        conect.Dispose();
        endresult = "Error while loading all employees. " + ex.ToString();
    }
}
// this method/Function displays an employee information for updates
private void get_EmployceInfo()
{
    endresult = " ";
    sqlStmt = "SELECT UserName, UserPswd, FirstName, MiddleName, LastName, " +
                "ContactPhone, Gender, EmailAddress, BirthDate, EmergencyPhone, " +
                "UserStatus, Remarks FROM EmpProfileTable " +
                "WHERE UserName = '" + UserName + "'";
    SqlConnection conect = new SqlConnection(MiscClass.dbaseConnect);
    SqlCommand cmd = new SqlCommand(sqlStmt, conect);
    SqlDataReader reader;
```

```
    try
    {
        conect.Open();
        reader = cmd.ExecuteReader();
        if (reader.Read())
        {
            userNameTxt.Text = reader ["UserName"].ToString();
            pswdTxt.Text = reader ["UserPswd"].ToString();
            fnameTxt.Text = reader["FirstName"].ToString();
            mnameTxt.Text = reader["MiddleName"].ToString();
            lnameTxt.Text = reader["LastName"].ToString();
            genderList.Text = reader["Gender"].ToString();
            phoneTxt.Text = reader["ContactPhone"].ToString();
            emailTxt.Text = reader["EmailAddress"].ToString();
            dobTxt.Text = reader["BirthDate"].ToString();
            emergencyPhoneTxt.Text = reader["EmergencyPhone"].ToString();
            empStatusList.Text = reader["UserStatus"].ToString();
            remarksTxt.Text = reader["Remarks"].ToString();
        }
        conect.Dispose();
        return;
    }
    catch (Exception ex)
    {
        conect.Dispose();
        endresult = "Error Reading EmpProfileTable. " + ex.ToString();
    }
}
// this is the Cancel Button Click event handler
private void cancelButton_Click(object sender, EventArgs e)
{
    this.Close();
}
// this is the Delete or Reset Button Click event handler
private void deleteResetButton_Click(object sender, EventArgs e)
{
    if (deleteResetButton.Text == "Reset")
    {
        init_Stuff();
        return;
    }
    delete_ExistingEmployee();
}
// This method/Function deletes an employee from database
```

```csharp
private void delete_ExistingEmployee()
{
    sqlStmt = "DELETE FROM EmpProfileTable WHERE UserName = '" + UserName + "'";
    SqlConnection conect = new SqlConnection(MiscClass.dbaseConnect);
    SqlCommand cmd = new SqlCommand(sqlStmt, conect);
    try
    {
        conect.Open();
        cmd.ExecuteNonQuery();
        conect.Dispose();
    }
    catch (Exception ex)
    {
        conect.Dispose();
        MessageBox.Show("Error while deleting a record. " + ex.ToString());
    }
}
// this is the go button Click event handler
private void goButton_Click(object sender, EventArgs e)
{
    if (goButton.Text == MiscClass.goButton)
    {
        add_NewEmployee();
        if (endresult != " ")
        {
            MessageBox.Show(endresult);
        }
        return;
    }
    update_ExistingEmployee();
    if (endresult != " ")
    {
        MessageBox.Show(endresult);
    }
}
// this method/function adds a new employee to the Employee database
private void add_NewEmployee()
{
    endresult = " ";
    string empProfile = (fnameTxt.Text + " " + lnameTxt.Text +
    " [Phone: " + phoneTxt.Text + " ]");
    sqlStmt = "INSERT INTO EmpProfileTable (UserName, UserPswd, " +
    "FirstName, MiddleName, LastName, " +
    "ContactPhone, Gender, EmailAddress, BirthDate, EmergencyPhone, " +
```

```
        "UserStatus, Remarks, EmpProfile, CreateDate)" +
        "VALUES (@UserName, @UserPswd, @FirstName, @MiddleName, " +
        "@LastName, @ContactPhone, @Gender, @EmailAddress, " +
        "@BirthDate, @EmergencyPhone, @UserStatus, @Remarks, " +
        "@EmpProfile, @CreateDate)";
        SqlConnection conect = new SqlConnection(MiscClass.dbaseConnect);
        SqlCommand cmd = new SqlCommand(sqlStmt, conect);
        cmd.Parameters.Add("@UserName", SqlDbType.VarChar, 50).Value = userNameTxt.Text;
        cmd.Parameters.Add("@UserPswd", SqlDbType.VarChar, 50).Value = pswdTxt.Text;
        cmd.Parameters.Add("@FirstName", SqlDbType.VarChar, 50).Value = fnameTxt.Text;
        cmd.Parameters.Add("@MiddleName", SqlDbType.VarChar, 50).Value = mnameTxt.Text;
        cmd.Parameters.Add("@LastName", SqlDbType.VarChar, 50).Value = lnameTxt.Text;
        cmd.Parameters.Add("@ContactPhone", SqlDbType.VarChar, 50).Value = phoneTxt.Text;
        cmd.Parameters.Add("@Gender", SqlDbType.VarChar, 10).Value = genderList.Text;
        cmd.Parameters.Add("@EmailAddress", SqlDbType.VarChar, 50).Value = emailTxt.Text;
        cmd.Parameters.Add("@BirthDate", SqlDbType.VarChar, 50).Value = dobTxt.Text;
        cmd.Parameters.Add("@EmergencyPhone", SqlDbType.VarChar, 50).Value = emergencyPhoneTxt.Text;
        cmd.Parameters.Add("@UserStatus", SqlDbType.VarChar, 50).Value = empStatusList.Text;
        cmd.Parameters.Add("@Remarks", SqlDbType.Text).Value = remarksTxt.Text;
        cmd.Parameters.Add("@EmpProfile", SqlDbType.VarChar, 200).Value = empProfile;
        cmd.Parameters.Add("@CreateDate", SqlDbType.VarChar, 50).Value = DateTime.Now.ToString();
        try
        {
            conect.Open();
            cmd.ExecuteNonQuery();
            conect.Dispose();
        }
        catch (Exception ex)
        {
            conect.Dispose ();
            endresult = "Error Adding Record " + ex.ToString ();
        }
}
// This method/function updates employee information in the Employee database
private void update_ExistingEmployee()
{
    endresult = " ";
    string empProfile = (fnameTxt.Text + " " + lnameTxt.Text + " [Phone: " + phoneTxt.Text + " ]");
    sqlStmt = "UPDATE EmpProfileTable SET UserName = @UserName, UserPswd = @UserPswd, " +
            "FirstName = @FirstName, MiddleName = @MiddleName, LastName = @LastName, " +
            "ContactPhone = @ContactPhone, Gender = @Gender, EmailAddress = @EmailAddress, " +
            "EmergencyPhone = @EmergencyPhone, UserStatus = @UserStatus, " +
            "Remarks = @Remarks  WHERE UserName = '" + UserName + "'";
    SqlConnection conect = new SqlConnection(MiscClass.dbaseConnect);
```

```
        SqlCommand cmd = new SqlCommand(sqlStmt, conect);
        cmd.Parameters.Add("@UserName", SqlDbType.VarChar, 50).Value = userNameTxt.Text;
        cmd.Parameters.Add("@UserPswd", SqlDbType.VarChar, 50).Value = pswdTxt.Text;
        cmd.Parameters.Add("@FirstName", SqlDbType.VarChar, 50).Value = fnameTxt.Text;
        cmd.Parameters.Add("@MiddleName", SqlDbType.VarChar, 50).Value = mnameTxt.Text;
        cmd.Parameters.Add("@LastName", SqlDbType.VarChar, 50).Value = lnameTxt.Text;
        cmd.Parameters.Add("@ContactPhone", SqlDbType.VarChar, 50).Value = phoneTxt.Text;
        cmd.Parameters.Add("@Gender", SqlDbType.VarChar, 10).Value = genderList.Text;
        cmd.Parameters.Add("@EmailAddress", SqlDbType.VarChar, 50).Value = emailTxt.Text;
        cmd.Parameters.Add("@BirthDate", SqlDbType.VarChar, 50).Value = dobTxt.Text;
        cmd.Parameters.Add("@EmergencyPhone", SqlDbType.VarChar, 50).Value = emergencyPhoneTxt.Text;
        cmd.Parameters.Add("@UserStatus", SqlDbType.VarChar, 50).Value = empStatusList.Text;
        cmd.Parameters.Add("@Remarks", SqlDbType.Text).Value = remarksTxt.Text;
        cmd.Parameters.Add("@EmpProfile", SqlDbType.VarChar, 200).Value = empProfile;
        try
        {
            conect.Open();
            cmd.ExecuteNonQuery();
            conect.Dispose();
        }
        catch (System.Exception ex)
        {
            conect.Dispose();
            endresult = "Error Updating Record " + ex.ToString();
        }
    }
    // This is the Help label Click event handler
    private void helpLabelTxt_Click(object sender, EventArgs e)
    {
        MessageBox.Show("Help Function not implemented yet - try next time ....");
    }
    // This is the Sign Out label Click event handler
    private void signOutLabelTxt_Click(object sender, EventArgs e)
    {
        this.Close();
    }
  } // end of ProfileForm class
} // end of WindowsApp namespace
```

STARTUP.CS

Program.cs is a default program that Visual Studio and the .Net Framework provide when you decide to create a Windows application based on them, because it's the entry point to the Windows Operating System to run/execute your application. You can always modify the name and content of 'Program.cs' to meet your needs. In this project, you decide to rename 'Program.cs' as 'StartUp.cs' and changed the 'Program' class to 'StartUp' and modified its content. The following is the source code of 'StartUp.cs':

```
using System;
using System.Collections.Generic;
using System.Linq;
using System.Data.SqlClient;
using System.Windows.Forms;
namespace WindowsApp
{
  static class StartUp
  {
      // this is the operating system entry point to run our application
      static void Main()
      {
            Application.EnableVisualStyles();
            Application.SetCompatibleTextRenderingDefault(false);
            string compRegistered = " ";
            verify_CompanyRegistration(compRegistered);
            if (compRegistered == "yes")
                Application.Run(new MainForm());
            else
                Application.Run(new InstallForm());
      }
      // this method verifies whether the client has registered
      private static string verify_CompanyRegistration(string compReg)
      {
          string sqlStmt = "SELECT CompanyName FROM CompProfileTable";
          SqlConnection conect = new SqlConnection(MiscClass.dbaseConnect);
          SqlCommand cmd = new SqlCommand(sqlStmt, conect);
          SqlDataReader reader;
          try
          {
              conect.Open();
              reader = cmd.ExecuteReader();
              if (reader.Read())
              {
```

```
            compReg = "yes";
        }
        conect.Dispose();
    }
    catch (Exception ex)
    {
        conect.Dispose();
        MessageBox.Show("Error while verifying company info. " + ex.ToString());
    }
    return compReg;
    }
 } // end of StartUp.cs class
} // end of WindowsApp namespace
```

WHAT HAVE YOU LEARNED?

- Applications developed using Windows programming are installed directly onto the device that uses them.

- Generally, these applications will have a single intended device (computer, tablet, or phone).

- You can drag in various elements from the 'Toolbox' to populate your application with.

- This type of programming is ideal for sale to organizations for internal use.

CHAPTER 9

WHAT IS BASIC INTERNET PROGRAMMING?

Internet programming is the process of creating an application system that can be used by an unlimited number of users across the globe. Internet programming is an extremely large improvement on using a Windows local area network. It's also described as a client/server application, just like a Window's client server application in a local area network setup environment to manage an organization's unique business operations. On the other hand, the client/server concept of the Internet application system is that the whole world is a client to any application on any global server(s). You can view the Internet as a group of local area networks working together by exchanging data and messages through parameters managed by global network systems to make information available to clients across the globe at the right time. The major difference between Windows applications and Internet applications is that there is no consistent link between the client and the server. Once a 'Page' is dispatched based on a client request, the link is disconnected instantly. This approach allows the server to respond to several clients simultaneously. That's the reason you can leave a 'Page' on all the time.

SERVER AND CLIENT

In the world of the Internet, a server is a special computer machine that keeps and maintains internet applications. These applications are like the applications on your personal computer or on a computer acting as a server in an organization's windows local area network environment. The only difference between a computer server and an Internet server, is that the Internet server is never turned off/shut down since the applications on those server(s) are accessed by clients from around the world twenty-four hours a day. Therefore, the 'Client' is any device that accesses the application on the remote server without knowing the location of the server. Sample clients for an Internet server are mainframe computers, mini-computers, desktops, laptops, tablets, mobile/handset devices, etc.

BROWSER, HTML AND PAGES

A browser is a special computer program (application) that allows information accessed by a client from a specific server to be displayed on the client device. These browser applications are created by Internet service providers. At the time of writing this book, some of the most common browsers are Internet Explorer, Edge, Chrome, Safari, and Firefox. The programming language the browser uses to display information is HTML (hypertext markup language). The information displayed by the browser is an instance of a user-defined data type called 'class' in an application somewhere on a server.

DOMAIN NAME AND UNIVERSAL RESOURCE LOCATOR (URL)

A domain name is a unique identifier used by the Internet to locate specific information on the web. It is often called an IP Address (Internet Protocol Address) on servers and is registered to the Domain Name System (DNS). The Universal Resource Locator (the URL) is like a house address. It gives complete directions to a specific 'class' in an application on a server somewhere. For instance, if you type *www.grg.com\register.aspx*, you're requesting an instance of a 'class' called 'register.aspx' from an application, so the 'Page' that you see is an 'object'.

HTTP (HYPERTEXT TRANSPORT/TRANSFER PROTOCOL)

The Hypertext Transport/Transfer Protocol (HTTP) is an application program that creates a network protocol used to send information from a computer server to clients across the globe. It can only carry hypertext information because that's the only language the browser can use to display information. Think of HTTP like an aircraft using the sky to carry cargo, a ship using the sea to carry cargo, or a truck using the road to carry goods to specific locations. The cargo/goods are a parceled 'HTML Page' and that page is an instance of a 'class' (i.e., object) in an application. HTTP doesn't care about or know the content of the information being carried/sent.

INTERNET PROGRAMMING USING ASP.NET AND C#.NET

ASP stands for Active Server Pages. The Microsoft .NET research group decided to create an Internet programming approach that's just like the Windows programming approach. ASP.NET is therefore an application that collaborates with the .NET Framework and Visual Studio to provide a complete, world-class enterprise Internet application development process. The ASP.NET application removes all the network complexities of Internet programming to allow the programmer to concentrate on the logic of application development.

ASP.NET uses 'Web Forms' to create a user interface called 'Pages' on the Internet in the same way you use 'Windows Forms' in Windows programming to create user interfaces popularly known as windows. ASP.NET uses 'Server and HTML Controls' in a Toolbox the same way you use 'User Interface Controls' in a Toolbox in Windows programming.

WEB FORMS, TOOLBOX, PROPERTIES, EVENTS AND EVENT HANDLERS

Visual Studio and the ASP.NET environment provide all the pieces you need to create an enterprise Web Application System. It uses 'Web Forms' to create 'Pages', just like 'Windows Forms' are used to create Windows applications. The 'Web Form' has three files, the design file, the source file that represents the Toolbox Server and HTML user-interface controls, and the program (i.e. the source code with the logic behind the 'Page'). The Web Form that acts as a 'Page/Container' for Server Controls like 'button', textbox, label, etc., is an instance of a Web Form 'class (i.e., object)'. The content of the Toolbox contains server controls and the controls that you drag and drop on a Web Form are also instances of the server control 'classes (i.e., objects)'.

Since Web Forms and the Toolbox Server Controls are 'classes', you use the properties of those objects to describe the characteristics of the objects. You also use events like 'click', 'mousehover', etc. and respond to the event by using handlers/methods.

SAMPLE WEB APPLICATION SYSTEM DEVELOPMENT PROCESS

Now that you understand the concept and methodology behind Internet programming, let's create a very simple Internet application and sell it to organizations that want to advertise themselves to the whole world. Everyone in the world can visit the organization's website, if they know the website address or the organization's name, by searching using any search engine like Google, Bing, etc.

This is a customized application, thus only one organization will use it to tell the world about itself, its products, and its services. Therefore, you'll only create three generic pages/classes as follows and will modify the page contents for clients based on their request:

- Home Page – (to welcome anyone that visits the website)
- About Us – (to introduce the organization to the world)
- Products and Services – (to explain to the world what the organization does)

Fortunately, Microsoft Visual Studio, in collaboration with the .NET Framework and ASP.NET application using the C# language, make it extremely easy for us to create a world-class Internet application with minimal effort. Visual Studio has some basic built-in Internet programming templates that can be used to start developing Internet applications. To start this application, let's launch the 'Microsoft Visual Web Developer 2010 Express' or whichever version you have installed on your computer as stated in the 'Systems Requirements' in this book. From the 'Start Page', click on 'New Project...' From the 'New Project' window, select 'Visual C#' and focus on 'Web', then choose 'ASP.NET Web Application. Name your project 'internetApp', and click 'OK'. Visual Studio automatically generates certain pages for you.

MASTER PAGE

ASP.NET uses the default master page to create uniform standard controls that appear on all the pages of your application for you. The master page acts as a container for all the pages in the application. The master page is the only file that contains the 'HTML' open and close tags. For instance, to have the same image/audio/video on all the pages of your application, you use the 'Site.master' class. You can always modify the default pages/classes that ASP.NET and Visual Studio provide. In this project, modify the 'Site.master' file by clicking on the 'split' option at the bottom of the source code and open the 'Toolbox'. You'll see the following environment:

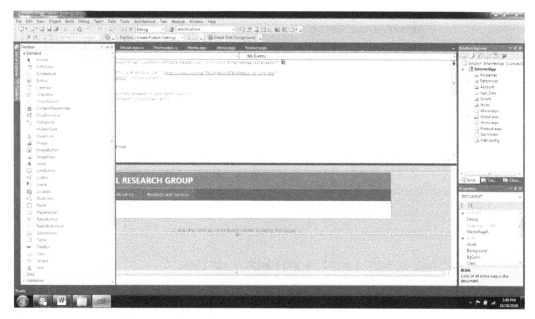

Figure 1. Master Page (Site.master) - Split View with Design and Source

The following is the HTML source for the above modified Site.Master page:

```
<%@ Master Language="C#" AutoEventWireup="true" CodeBehind="Site.master.cs"
Inherits="InternetApp.SiteMaster" %>
<!DOCTYPE html PUBLIC "-//W3C//DTD XHTML 1.0 Strict//EN" "http://www.w3.org/TR/
xhtml1/DTD/xhtml1-strict.dtd">
<html xmlns="http://www.w3.org/1999/xhtml" xml:lang="en">
<head runat="server">
  <title></title>
  <link href="~/Styles/Site.css" rel="stylesheet" type="text/css" />
  <asp:ContentPlaceHolder ID="HeadContent" runat="server">
  </asp:ContentPlaceHolder>
</head>
<body>
  <form runat="server">
  <div class="page">
    <div class="header">
      <div class="title">
        <h1>
          Global Research Group
        </h1>
      </div>
      <div class="clear hideSkiplink">
        <asp:Menu ID="NavigationMenu" runat="server" CssClass="menu"
EnableViewState="false" IncludeStyleBlock="false" Orientation="Horizontal">
```

```
                <Items>
                    <asp:MenuItem NavigateUrl="~/Home.aspx" Text="Home"/>
                    <asp:MenuItem NavigateUrl="~/About.aspx" Text="About Us"/>
                    <asp:MenuItem NavigateUrl="~/Product.aspx" Text="Products and
Services"/>
                </Items>
            </asp:Menu>
        </div>
    </div>
    <div class="main">
        <asp:ContentPlaceHolder ID="MainContent" runat="server"/>
    </div>
    <div class="clear">
    </div>
  </div>
  <div class="footer">
    <h6>
    ..... building bridges of research work accross the globe .....
    </h6>
  </div>
  </form>
</body>
</html>
```

The following is the default program (source code) provided by Visual Studio for the Site. master.cs class (i.e., the code behind). You can always modify this program to manage the Master Page contents in your application. To see this program, click 'View' on the menu bar and select 'Code'. This is where you code all the logic to manage your application. Most of your code here will be event handlers (the same as the event handlers in your Windows application in chapter 8) and methods.

```
using System;
using System.Collections.Generic;
using System.Linq;
using System.Web;
using System.Web.UI;
using System.Web.UI.WebControls;
namespace InternetApp
{
  public partial class SiteMaster : System.Web.UI.MasterPage
  /* SiteMaster class inherits MasterPage class */
  {
      protected void Page_Load(object sender, EventArgs e)
      {
      }
  }
}
```

HOME PAGE

The following is the split view of the design and source of the Home.aspx class file with the 'Toolbox' window to drag and drop 'Server/HTML' controls:

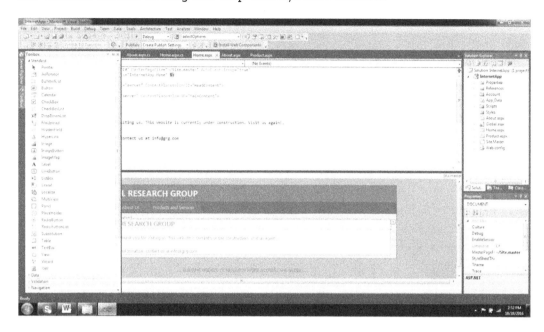

Figure 2. Home.aspx Source and Design View

The following is the modified Home.aspx source:

```
<%@ Page Title="Home Page" Language="C#" MasterPageFile="~/Site.master"
AutoEventWireup="true"
  CodeBehind="Home.aspx.cs" Inherits="InternetApp.Home" %>
<asp:Content ID="HeaderContent" runat="server" ContentPlaceHolderID="HeadContent">
</asp:Content>
<asp:Content ID="BodyContent" runat="server" ContentPlaceHolderID="MainContent">
  <h2>
        Global Research Group
  </h2>
  <p>
        Welcome and thank you for visiting us. This website is currently under construction.
Visit us again!.
  </p>
  <p>
        For additional information, contact us at info@grg.com
  </p>
```

```
</asp:Content>
```
The following is the default source code for the Home.aspx.cs page/class. You can always modify this class (source code) to manage the home page user interface.
```
using System;
using System.Collections.Generic;
using System.Linq;
using System.Web;
using System.Web.UI;
using System.Web.UI.WebControls;
namespace InternetApp
{
  public partial class Home : System.Web.UI.Page
  {
    protected void Page_Load(object sender, EventArgs e)
    {
    }
  }
}
```

Now click 'Debug' on the menu bar and select "Start Debugging', you'll see the following home page:

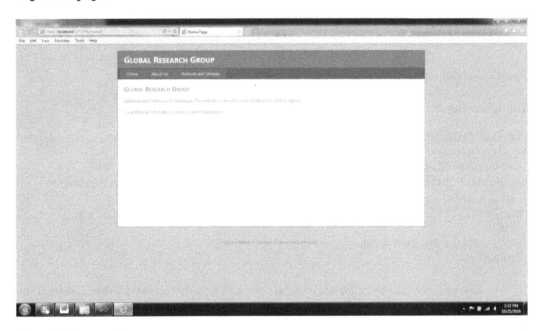

Figure 3. Home.aspx Page

ABOUT.ASPX

The following is the split view of design and source of the About.aspx page:

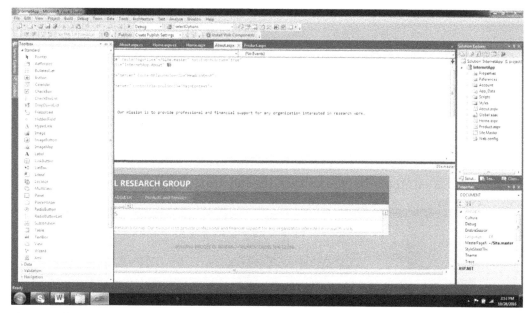

Figure 4. About.aspx Split View with Design and Source

The following is the source code of About.aspx page/class design:

```
<%@ Page Title="About Us" Language="C#" MasterPageFile="~/Site.master"
AutoEventWireup="true"
  CodeBehind="About.aspx.cs"  Inherits="InternetApp.About" %>
<asp:Content ID="HeaderContent" runat="server" ContentPlaceHolderID="HeadContent">
</asp:Content>
<asp:Content ID="BodyContent" runat="server" ContentPlaceHolderID="MainContent">
  <h2>
     About Us
  </h2>
  <p>
        We are Global Research Group. Our mission is to provide professional and financial
        support for any organization interested in research work.
  </p>
</asp:Content>
```

The following is the source code for About.aspx.cs (i.e., the code behind the page):

```
using System;
using System.Collections.Generic;
```

```
using System.Linq;
using System.Web;
using System.Web.UI;
using System.Web.UI.WebControls;
namespace InternetApp
{
  public partial class About : System.Web.UI.Page
  {
    protected void Page_Load(object sender, EventArgs e)
    {
    }
  }
}
```

When you click on 'About Us' you will see the following page:

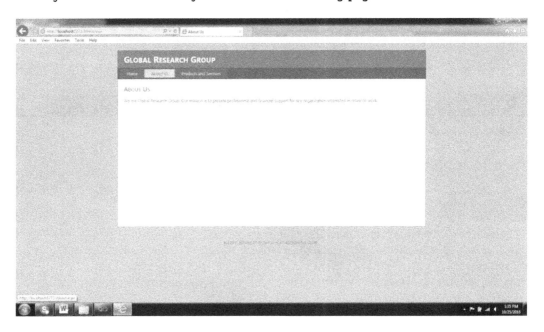

Figure 5. About.aspx Page.

PRODUCT.ASPX

The following is the split view of design and source of the Product.aspx page:

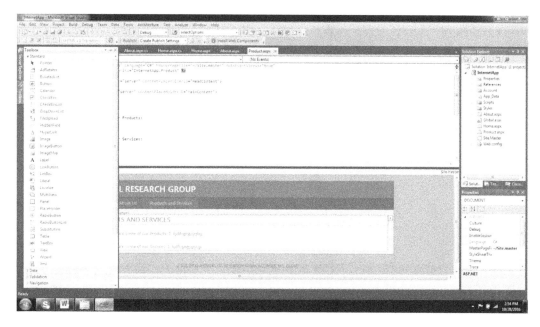

Figure 6. Product.aspx Split View with Design and Source

The following is the source code of Product.aspx page design:

```
<%@ Page Title="Products and Services" Language="C#" MasterPageFile="~/Site.master" A
utoEventWireup="true" CodeBehind="Product.aspx.cs" Inherits="InternetApp.Product" %>
<asp:Content ID="HeaderContent" runat="server" ContentPlaceHolderID="HeadContent">
</asp:Content>
<asp:Content ID="BodyContent" runat="server" ContentPlaceHolderID="MainContent">
  <h2>
    Products and Services
  </h2>
  <p>
    The following are some of our Products:
    1. kjdfkgjkgjjggkgj
  </p>
  <p>
    The following are some of our Services:
    1. kjdfkgjkgjjggkgj
  </p>
</asp:Content>
```

The following is the source code for Product.aspx.cs (i.e. the code behind):

```
using System;
using System.Collections.Generic;
using System.Linq;
using System.Web;
using System.Web.UI;
using System.Web.UI.WebControls;
namespace InternetApp
{
  public partial class Product : System.Web.UI.Page
  {
    protected void Page_Load(object sender, EventArgs e)
    {
    }
  }
}
```

When you click on products and services, you'll see the following page:

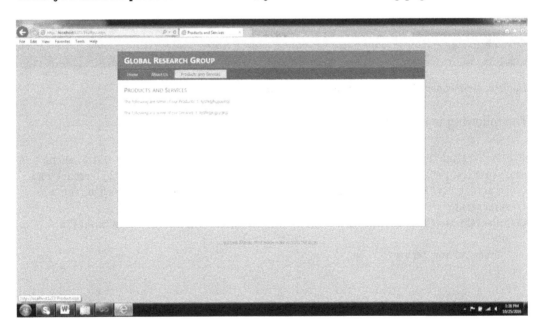

Figure 7. Product.aspx Page

WHAT HAVE YOU LEARNED?

- Internet programming is used to create applications that can be used and accessed by an unlimited number of users.

- Instead of being stored on a Local Area Network, these applications are stored on a server that can be accessed by the client from any location.

- Web browsers use HTML and CSS to display web applications.

CHAPTER 10

CONCLUSION

Information technology is a broad discipline. It has many specializations like computer science, software engineering, information security, systems design and analysis, and database administration that work together to create applications that serve a useful purpose. This has made IT an integral part of our lives. Without any formal education, users all over the world use applications on their phones to perform important tasks, like booking travel.

However, many curious people, like you, want a deeper understanding of how computers and other devices work. Without the time or resources to go to college, a book like this one can go a long way toward learning about IT. These skills can help you join the growing group of IT contributors instead of staying a consumer.

For our conclusion, let's review what you've learned in each section. This will refresh your memory and show you which points you might need to work on further.

PART ONE: INTRODUCING COMPUTER PROGRAMMING

In this section, you learned the basic theoretical concepts and features of computer programming. The following three chapters explained and taught you the fundamentals of becoming a computer programmer/software developer through practical examples.

CHAPTER 1

This chapter explains what makes computers work. Here you learned about the software that works together to make computers work. The software that works together to make the computer function and meet the user's goals includes the following:

- Operating System: the resident software that manages all the resources on the computer and supports application system usability.

- Compiler, Interpreter, and Translator: software that translates source codes (programs) into machine language.

- Machine Language: the only language the computer understands (binary code or format). This is the output/result of compiler/interpreter functions.

- Device Drivers: unique programs that support external peripheral devices, such as a printer or camera.

This chapter also compared the different kinds of computer programmers, including:

- Systems Programmers: programmers that create systems software, such as Operating Systems, Device Drivers, and Database Management Systems.

- Applications Programmers: programmers that create real-life application systems like banking, insurance, and airline reservation application systems.

- Software Developers: any computer programmer is a software developer. This is just a recent title within the IT departments of organizations.

CHAPTER 2

In this chapter, you learned what a programming language is by comparing them to a human language like English. Different programming approaches and the characteristics of a typical programming language were also explained. A few of the things you learned were:

- The most common parts of a programming language like, Syntax, Semantics, Lexical Structure, Data Types, Primitive Data Type, User-Defined Data Types, Value Types, and Reference Types were explained with examples.

- The difference between procedural-oriented programming languages and object-oriented programming languages were explained with examples.

- Characteristics shared by most programming languages, such as keywords, arithmetical and logical operations identifiers (symbols), variable declaration, constant declaration, data structure/collection (structure/record, array and list) declaration, assignment statement, input statements, output statements, conditional statements, looping statements, transfer statements, functions and comment declarations were explained with examples. This is the most important information in this book, because if you know the characteristics of a programming language, then you can easily learn any programming language and choose the language you would like to develop your application system/software product with.

CHAPTER 3

In chapter 2 you learned the basics of programming languages, so this chapter dove deeper into computer programming as a process for writing a computer program to create an application system/software product using a specific programming language. Every application system/software product is created with a specific programming language. The Microsoft C#.NET programming language was used as a case study to teach the reader how to write a computer program using the characteristics of a programming language as explained in chapter 2. The following features of developing software using C#.NET were explained through extensive examples:

- The .NET Framework is a class library and a run-time support system that manages all the programming languages that target the .NET system including C#.

- The basics of C#.NET programming were shown using the following programming parts along with detailed explanations and practical examples:

  - C# built-in primitive data types, using arrays and collections in C#, C# user-defined data types.

  - The 'class' user-defined data type definition and declaration, class members, class accessibility, class instances, class and inheritance, static, sealed, and abstract class definitions and declarations.

  - Virtual method, overridden method and overloaded method definitions, declarations, and usage.

  - Structure user-defined data types, exception user-defined data types, and enumerations user-defined data type definitions, declarations, and usage.

- C# keywords, operator identifiers (symbols), program control flow, iteration (looping) statements, conditional statements and control transfer statements.

- The purpose of the Microsoft Visual Studio Software development tool was provided along with all of the procedures you need to create an application system. You learned how the Visual Studio collaborates with the .NET Framework to provide a RAD (rapid application development) environment. You also learned how to develop, test, debug and run your program with examples.

PART TWO: INTRODUCING APPLICATION SYSTEM DEVELOPMENT

In this section, you learned the basic processes/steps for developing an application system/software product.

CHAPTER 4

This chapter continued to build on the basics you've learned by helping you to create an application. It provided you with the basics of the application system development process. The following approach was used as a case study for the guidelines:

- You must know what application system you want to create (i.e., target and scope – your audience). For instance, an application system to manage your bills.

- Choose a programming language and a software development environment/tool that can support your development process.

- Choose a hardware platform and the operating system for the project.

- Analyze and design the system. What application type will it be? A console application, a Windows application, Internet application, or a mobile application? What data access type should you use (file system or database management system)? What is the input, processing, and output criteria? Use a program flowchart to guide the flow of your logic.

- Write the program, test, and debug; if there are errors fix them. Implement/deploy your application to your audience.

PART THREE: INTRODUCING PROGRAMMING AND DATA ACCESS

Every application uses some form of data. This section explains what data access is and how it is used in programming. The chapter then provides the reader with the two most common data access methods, the File System and the Relational Database Management System.

CHAPTER 5

This chapter thoroughly explains the File System and how you can dynamically manage the File System in a program. The following features were used to teach you how to access data in a program using the File System:

- The 'Path' System, the address to your data's location.

- C#.NET and Data Access using the File System.

- How to create a directory/sub-directory (folder), how to create a file in a directory, how to open a file, how to write a record to a file, how to read a record from a file, how to close a file, how to delete a file from a directory/folder, and how to delete a directory/sub-directory (folder).

CHAPTER 6

This chapter explains the meaning and purpose of database management systems as a software that bridges the gap between a program and a data store. The Relational Database Management System (RDBMS), among others, was used to teach you the high-level representation of data as perceived by RDBMS. The chapter explains the meaning of the following with practical examples:

- Structured Query Language (SQL) is the language used by the Relational Database Management System to define the database and manipulate the data in the database tables. Statements like CREATE, DROP, DELETE, INSERT, UPDATE, and SELECT were explained with examples.

- You learned how to use the 'classes' in ADO.NET with the C#.NET as a case study for the following samples: how to create a database, how to create a table, how to add a new record to a table, how to update record(s) in a table, how to read record(s) in a table, how to delete record(s) in a table, how to delete a table and how to delete a database.

PART FOUR: DIFFERENT KINDS OF PROGRAMMING

This section provides you with practical examples using the three most popular approaches in programming. It also showed how your choices would be affected based on the application that you decided to develop.

CHAPTER 7

This chapter introduced you to console programming. Here you also learned about the first programming system (i.e. the "Card Punch" system) and how console programming used "Terminals" to extend and replaced the "Card Punch" programming system. The reader also learned that this is the best starting point to learn computer programming, since the programmer interacts directly with the computer machine using the services of an operating system. The C#.NET programming language and the services of Visual Studio and the .NET Framework were used to create an example of a console application system.

CHAPTER 8

In this chapter, you learned about Windows programming. You also learned the difference between console and Windows programming, and how Windows programming extended console programming. The C#.NET, Visual Studio Development Environment and the .NET Framework Class Library services were used to create a practical Windows application. The following features were explained and applied:

- Windows Forms, Toolbox, properties, events and event handlers
- Sample Windows application system development process
- Windows application system analysis and design
- Windows application system implementation/deployment process

CHAPTER 9

Basic Internet programming is explained in this chapter. The main differences between Windows and Internet programming were explained. The following features in Internet programming were explained:

- Server and client
- Browser, HTML, and pages

- Domain name and universal resource locator (URL)
- HTTP (hypertext transport/transfer protocol)

The Microsoft ASP.NET Internet development tool was used to create a very simple Internet application system. This chapter explained how you use web forms to create pages, the same way that you use Windows forms to create windows. The following features were explained and applied:

- Web Forms, Toolbox, properties, events and event handlers
- Sample Internet application system development process

Now that you've finished reading this book, you will be able to create any application system you like and even market your own unique software products. And the biggest benefit you've received is knowing the characteristics of a programming language. With this skill you can easily learn any programming language and use it to create your very own application.

With lots of practice, and this book as a guide and reference, you can eventually seek a position as an entry-level computer programmer/software developer in any organization. Also, if you're already working in an organization with an IT department, you can easily transfer to that department if you're interested.

You can always reach me at *support@asiotech.net* for any question regarding this book. Also, visit the following website to subscribe and get information about our books with similar content *http://www.asiotech.net/subscribe*. When you subscribe, you'll receive our newsletter, magazines, updates on new books, software development learning materials and more, all for **FREE**. I wish you the best in your journey to be part of the growing group of application and software evelopers!

ABOUT THE AUTHOR

Sam Hinton is a software architect and a software engineering consultant. He has over twenty years of IT teaching and industry experience. This includes outstanding experience in software/application systems development for the Microsoft Windows, UNIX/Linux and IBM AS/400 environments. He also has experience in technical writing, project leadership, web-enabled and rich client application systems development, database administration, systems conversion and integration. Sam Hinton works as a consultant with several companies in Canada and the United States (especially in the Tri-State area of New Jersey, New York and Connecticut), this experience is mainly with Wall Street companies. He's an expert in core Java, core C#.NET, and the object-oriented design and programming methodology. Currently, he applies Microsoft.NET development technologies with C#.NET to training and teaching software developers. Sam Hinton holds Bachelor of Science degree in Computer Science from University of Science and Technology in Ghana and Master of Science degree in Computation from McMaster University, Hamilton in Ontario Canada. He is the co-founder of Asio Technologies [www.asiotech.net]. He can be contacted at *support@asiotech.net*.

www.ingramcontent.com/pod-product-compliance
Lightning Source LLC
Chambersburg PA
CBHW080553060326
40689CB00021B/4842